The Bride-to-Bride Book

A Complete Wedding Planner for the Bride

Your Step-by-Step Guide to a Perfect Wedding Day

Pamela A. Piljac

For Tom, whose ideas, support, encouragement, and assistance made this book possible.

A special thank you to all the brides who helped by sharing their ideas, experiences, and suggestions. I am especially grateful to Laurie Grace, Carol Gust, Cheryl Hines, Barbara Krga, Jennifer T. Lach, Jennifer Pielow, Karen Rowlett, Linda Sims, and Florence Zavacky.

This book was written to provide a variety of information that will assist in the task of wedding planning. It provides educational and background information, and is sold with the understanding that it does not contain all of the information available on any given subject. Regulations, practices, customs, and methods will vary. Advice offered must be weighed with that in mind. Although the author has made every effort to be as accurate as possible, mistakes in content or typographical errors may still exist. The author and/or Bryce-Waterton Publications will not be liable or responsible to any person or entity with respect to any loss or damage caused or alleged to be caused, directly, or indirectly, by the information contained in this book.

---

10 9 8 7 6 5 4 3 2

The Bride to Bride Book: A Complete Wedding Planner for the Bride
Copyright © 1989, Pamela A. Piljac. All rights reserved. No part of this book may be reproduced in any form, or by any electronic or mechanical means, including information storage or retrieval systems, without the express written consent of the publisher. Some information contained in this book was originally copyrighted © in 1983, and 1987. Published by Bryce-Waterton Publications, 6411 Mulberry Avenue, Portage, IN 46368

Library of Congress Cataloging in Publication Data

Piljac, Pamela A.,   1954-
2. Wedding etiquette I. Title
X

ISBN 0-913339-08-3

PRINTED IN THE UNITED STATES OF AMERICA

Foreword

Congratulations! This is an exciting time for you! Planning a wedding is more than just preparing for the happy occasion; it's a time to adjust to your new roles and lives together. With so much to consider, and so many choices, each decision will be another step toward your future happiness.

A wedding is a time for making memories. Each of us has her own idea of the type of day she wants it to be. In this book I try to present both sides of each traditional option, as well as additional ideas to consider. I'll draw on the personal experiences of others to let you know what to expect. My hope is that this knowledge will help you make your day a perfect one.

This book will inform you, discussing even the smallest part of the wedding in detail. It'll assist you in making those difficult decisions. There are times when it might make you laugh—such as when you learn the origins of some wedding customs. It should also make you think, not only about the wedding, but about your future lives together.

There are charts for easy reference, and worksheets to help you obtain the information you need and use it to your best advantage. There are sections to help you keep records and make plans. It's all designed to tell you what you need to know in order to organize and plan the best wedding possible for your budget.

This is the book I wish I would have had when preparing for my marriage. There are plenty of other books around that simply give you another person's opinion about weddings in general, or assume you're well-to-do and care a great deal about the finer points of etiquette. But, for the average woman with limited funds who needs help in planning her own 'perfect' wedding, this book is for you!

Table of Contents

INTRODUCTION 1

SECTION 1: *Before You Begin Planning* 3

GETTING STARTED 3
COUNTDOWN TO THE WEDDING DAY 4
GETTING READY FOR MARRIAGE 7
ANNOUNCEMENTS 14
RINGS 15
MONETARY RESPONSIBILITIES 17
BUDGET 19
101 MONEY SAVING TIPS 23
PRE-WEDDING PARTIES 27
OTHER BRIDES TALK ABOUT THEIR WEDDINGS 28
DISASTERS AND MISHAPS 38

SECTION 2: *Making Basic Decisions* 41

WEDDING STYLES 41
SECOND MARRIAGE 42
TYPES OF CEREMONIES 43
PERSONALIZING YOUR CEREMONY 48
SELECTING THE CEREMONY SITE 49
SELECTING THE RECEPTION SITE 51
WEDDING CUSTOMS—WHERE DO THEY COME FROM? 52

SECTION 3: *Finishing Touches* 59

YOUR WEDDING PARTY 59
FINDING THE PERFECT DRESS 63
ACCESSORIES—THE FINISHING TOUCHES 76
CHOOSING ATTIRE FOR THE FEMALE ATTENDANTS 78
EVERYONE'S GUIDE TO WEDDING APPAREL 79
MEN'S FORMALWEAR 80
FLOWERS 83
BRIDAL REGISTRIES 86
GIFTS 87
INVITATIONS 89
GUEST LIST 103
PHOTOGRAPHER/VIDEO 106

SECTION 4: *Step by Step Guide to Planning the Details* 113

CEREMONY 113
RECEPTION 116
FOOD/CATERING 121
WEDDING CAKE 126
BEVERAGES 127
MUSIC AND MUSICIANS 129
TRANSPORTATION 132
SECURITY 134

SECTION 5: *The Big Last Day* 137

REHEARSAL 137
DELAY OR CANCELLATION 137
YOUR WEDDING DAY 139
HONEYMOON PLANNING 139

Introduction

A wedding can be very expensive, and a lot of work. You have to gather information, organize it, then put it into practice. You, your fiance, and both families will have different ideas and expectations about the style, size, and character of your celebration. You have to keep everyone happy, while making decisions that will create the wedding you want. Or you may not be sure what type of wedding to have, or what you can afford. You need assistance from the voices of experience—and you'll find them here.

Don't let someone else do everything for you. If you don't participate in the planning, it won't seem like your wedding. If you aren't sure exactly what you want, collect a scrapbook of clippings—pictures of gowns, headpieces, flowers, and formalwear that you like. After a while, a pattern will emerge that will make the decisions easier.

How do you find the information you need? First, you must locate quality business people to interview. Ask people who have recently married or put on large celebrations for recommendations. Then use the questionnaire sheets in each related section as a starting point for your interviews. Feel free to add additional questions. The right business operator for you will be the one that offers the things you want at the price you can afford—and has reliable references and reputation.

As you tell friends, relatives, and acquaintances about your upcoming plans you'll probably be showered with advice and opinions. Don't resent this as interference. Think of it as input from trusted advisors. It doesn't hurt to listen, but you certainly don't have to follow any advice that you don't feel comfortable with. This isn't always easy, especially when families are involved. You may feel torn between asserting your own ideas and beliefs and dealing with the customs and traditions of your family. Remember, it's only through understanding and compromise that the best weddings occur.

All the helpful information in the world can be meaningless if it's not properly utilized. Planning a wedding is a lot like running a corporation. You have to know a little about many different things to make the proper decisions. You must hire people to provide services for you. Most importantly, you must budget and co-ordinate the whole event without letting the little details slip away.

Record everything in one place: names, phone numbers, plans, ideas, appointments, and notes from conversations. Keep all the information in the same place at all times. This book has lists that will help you in setting goals, establishing priorities, delegating responsibilities, and keeping track of errands that must be done. You'll also need to create a few of your own, perhaps daily and weekly work lists to make sure everything stays on track. If you don't complete an item on schedule, transfer it to the next list. With so many distractions, it's very easy to forget important details. It's dangerous to try to remember everything—that's why writing it down is so important. One bride I know was so busy trying to find a dress and a caterer that she completely forgot about ordering flowers until two weeks before her wedding!

Plans don't mean a thing if they stay on paper. You have to act. No time for everything? Every manager knows that the first step to effective results is to delegate. Ask responsible people, whether it's your mother, sister, or maid of honor for help. They can assist with gathering information, or handling details such as addressing envelopes. Avoid misunderstandings and hurt feelings by clearly communicating what you expect of them, and when you need the results. Keep yourself free to look at information and make decisions.

For best results, have signed contracts with each of your service providers. That includes the florist, photographer, caterer, musicians, and anyone who is being paid to supply something on your wedding day. Call them a week or two before the wedding and confirm all details. If you signed the contract six months before, the business may have changed hands, moved, or encountered other problems. You want to deal with the issue ahead of time—not on the morning of your wedding.

Think about what might go wrong, and take steps to resolve the situation before it happens. Have a backup for every service in case one doesn't appear at the appointed time. Carry a card listing your second choice—or of those you know will be available on your wedding day. If something goes wrong, you'll have someone to call. Check around. Is there a major convention in town the weekend of your wedding? Call your local chamber of commerce if you're not sure. It could affect hotel accommodations, limousines, formalwear rental, and other services.

This is probably the first major endeavor that you and your fiance will pursue together. With all the work, feelings, and emotions involved there will certainly be arguments and disagreements. In fact, if there aren't, you should re-examine how well you are communicating. Sharing this project can be a good test of your relationship, and may reflect to some degree what your lives will be like after the wedding. However, don't panic if you are beginning to argue a lot more right now. Pre-wedding jitters affect nearly everyone. Most couples argue a great deal over trivial details before the wedding.

During the planning process, you'll probably go through several emotional phases. First, you'll be very excited and think and talk about weddings most of the time. You may even be a bit hurt and frustrated because your fiance, friends, and loved ones won't be as interested in the subject. Take advantage of your enthusiasm and use this time to gather information. Remember, midway through the planning you'll probably become very tired of the whole situation. All the details, decisions, problems, and emotions involved will wear you down. This is the point where you might go off your budget just to get decisions out of the way. It's the time when some couples give up and elope.

Make a mental note that when you reach this point it's time to STOP, take a day, and get away from it all. Don't think one thought or say one word about marriage, weddings, or your future. All of these problems have a solution, and they'll be resolved one at a time. You just need to step back and put it all in perspective. Millions of couples have experienced this and now recall their wedding with fond memories. That doesn't mean they didn't have problems. They've just eventually faded into the background, as yours will. Stick to it, and you'll have a lovely wedding day.

Generally, you will expect more from others than they can give you, and they will probably expect more from you than you can give them. Try to keep it all in perspective, and don't forget that it's just one day in your life!

Before You Begin Planning

Getting Started

We're ready to set the date. How soon should the wedding be held after we announce our engagement?

What kind of wedding do you want? A large wedding will take months to plan. Some religious denominations (such as Roman Catholic) require a pre-marital counseling period of six to twelve months before the ceremony. The date you set may depend on the availability of a certain hall, caterer, or band that you'd like to have. In the peak wedding months of June, July, and August, popular locations might already be reserved two years ahead of time. Your date should be one that fits into your mutual schedules, and allows you to have the type of wedding that you desire.

Who makes the final decisions? If my parents are paying the bills can they run the show?

This is your special day, and you should both feel comfortable at your own ceremony and reception. Control over the wedding plans is generally based on tradition, not on who contributes the most money. Based on that, the bride and groom, and then the bride's parents have the greatest say in the decisions. It's a good idea to sit down with everyone that will contribute financially and discuss the general plans. If your parents can't afford the wedding you want, you'll have to contribute the difference or pare down your plans. If money isn't the problem, just remember that compromises are essential, and disagreements are inevitable. It never hurts to LISTEN to ideas and suggestions. If monetary contributions will be issued with strings attached, it may be best to plan a wedding you can afford on your own.

How much does a wedding cost?

Whatever you want to spend. Other than the cost of state-required medical tests, a marriage license, and payment to the officiant who performs the ceremony, you needn't spend a dime. Where you marry, what you wear, the number of people in attendance, and the size of the following celebration can vary immensely. Generally, a formal wedding (see *Wedding Styles* section for definition of formal wedding) can start at $3,500 and run to $15,000 or more. Plan your wedding to fit your budget.

Who pays for what?

The chapter titled: *Monetary Responsibilities* offers a breakdown of the customary division of expenses. Traditionally, the bride's parents covered most of the bills. But today, these arrangements are quite flexible and many couples pay for the entire affair themselves; or fund it through a combination of contributors including both sets of parents, and relatives on both sides of the family. However, such contributions must be entirely voluntary, and you should never try to have a wedding that costs more than your contributors can comfortably afford.

We'd like to have our wedding bands engraved. What should they say?
If the band is wide enough you might have the wedding date, both sets of initials, and even a short meaningful phrase. Narrow bands are seldom engraved, but you may choose to have the date, or your initials etched in.

How do we obtain a marriage license?
The clerk's office in most counties handles the distribution of marriage licenses. Look in the phone book under the name of your county. There you will find a listing of government offices. Call and ask about State requirements, such as which blood and medical tests are necessary, the waiting time before and after the license is issued, age and residence requirements, and what paperwork is needed (such as identification, proof of citizenship, or proof of divorce). Turn to the *'Ceremony Details'* chapter for additional information.

Countdown to the Wedding Day

What do you need to do, and when does it have to be done? Here's a timing outline that covers wedding tasks. If you're having a big, formal wedding in a major metropolitan area, or during the peak wedding months of June, July, or August, you may need more time than this section indicates. In addition, some popular churches, caterers, and reception sites are reserved two or three years in advance. It is much better to start too early than too late. If you try to do everything at the last minute, you'll pay more, have fewer choices, and more headaches and anxiety.

Twelve Months Before
- ☐ Select engagement ring.
- ☐ Make general wedding decisions—date, style, size of guest list.
- ☐ Set a preliminary budget.
- ☐ Choose the location for the ceremony, and the officiant.
- ☐ Reserve the reception site.
- ☐ Learn about caterers, photographers, florists, musicians, and other service providers.
- ☐ Begin compiling guest list.

Six Months Before
- ☐ Ask your Maid of Honor, Bridesmaids, Flower Girl, and Ring Bearer, to join your wedding party.
- ☐ Announce your engagement in the newspapers.
- ☐ Select your dress, headpiece, and bridesmaid's gowns.
- ☐ Talk to your fiance about honeymoon destinations, make plans and reservations. Most popular spots are reserved early each year.
- ☐ If you're traveling abroad on your honeymoon, verify that your passport is up to date, and find out what inoculations are required.
- ☐ Place deposits and sign contracts for wedding services: such as photographer, florist, caterer, and musicians.

Four Months Before
- ☐ If your housing arrangements aren't settled, it's time to start looking for home furnishings and a place to live.
- ☐ Verify that your gown and the bridesmaid's dresses have been ordered.
- ☐ Make sure addresses for guest list are up to date, and that both families have compiled theirs. Organize the information.
- ☐ Order invitations, announcements, and any personal stationery.
- ☐ Confirm that your fiance has chosen and ordered his attire, and that all male attendants have ordered their formalwear.
- ☐ Verify that both mothers have selected/ordered their gowns.

- ☐ Check the requirements for medical tests/marriage license.
- ☐ Make appointment for physical exam/medical tests.
- ☐ Shop for trousseau.

Two Months Before

- ☐ Register at bridal registry. If you come from different towns, you should register at stores in both towns.
- ☐ Verify that all required documents (both civil and religious) are in order. For example: birth certificate, citizenship papers, proof of divorce, baptismal and confirmation certificates.
- ☐ Address the invitations and announcements. The invitations should be sent four to six weeks before the wedding, the announcements after the ceremony.
- ☐ Shop for gifts for groom and attendants.
- ☐ Choose wedding rings, arrange for engraving.
- ☐ Order wedding cake if it's not supplied by the caterer.
- ☐ Finalize and verify all details with service suppliers.
- ☐ Plan bridesmaid's luncheon.
- ☐ Schedule an appointment with your hairdresser for your wedding day.
- ☐ Complete honeymoon plans.
- ☐ Shop for accessories not yet purchased, such as purse, shoes, ring bearer's pillow, goblets, candles, guest book, cake knife, and garter.
- ☐ Shop for dresses you'll wear to showers, pre-wedding parties, and your 'Going Away' outfit.

Six Weeks Before

- ☐ Confirm all male and female attendants have been fitted for formalwear.
- ☐ Have formal bridal portrait done. Discuss wedding photo shots with photographer.
- ☐ Make final menu decisions.
- ☐ Mail invitations six to eight weeks before the wedding.
- ☐ Attend bridal and personal showers.
- ☐ Make sure transportation arrangements have been made for all attendants and important guests on the wedding day.
- ☐ Set rehearsal. Make sure all attendants are aware of the time and date.

Two Weeks Before

- ☐ Have bridesmaid's luncheon.
- ☐ Remind groom to get a haircut.
- ☐ Pick up your gown (if you didn't have a formal portrait). Be sure to try it on!
- ☐ Keep records of gifts as they arrive. Write Thank You notes immediately. Pre-address envelopes for Thank You notes to other guests.
- ☐ Verify security arrangements have been made for the reception.
- ☐ Make sure musicians have a list of your musical selections for the ceremony and reception.
- ☐ Take care of blood/medical tests, marriage license.
- ☐ Confirm accommodations reservations for out of town guests.
- ☐ If you'll be moving, fill out a change of address card at the Post Office.
- ☐ If you'll be using your new husband's name, collect the necessary forms for changing your driver's license, Social Security card, insurance policies, bank accounts, etc. Don't forget to change the beneficiary on insurance policies.
- ☐ Prepare wedding announcement for newspapers.
- ☐ Make seating chart for reception, even if it will only apply to head table. Make place cards for head table, and give them to the caterer.
- ☐ Address formal announcements, so they can be mailed on your wedding day.
- ☐ Arrange for person to say grace before dinner.
- ☐ Begin moving to your new residence.

One Week Before	☐ Pick up rings.
	☐ Give the final guest count for the reception to your caterer.
	☐ Practice applying makeup for the wedding day, using a white (or ivory) towel as background. If you'll be married outdoors, remember that lighting will be different. Practice in natural light.
	☐ Give attendants their gifts (or do this at the Rehearsal Dinner).
	☐ Verify all attendants have picked up and tried on their dresses.
	☐ Prepare ceremony seating list for ushers (if necessary).
	☐ Make a list of names and pronunciation for the Best Man to mention in his introduction.
	☐ Confirm honeymoon plans.
	☐ Pack for honeymoon.
	☐ Pay upcoming bills.
	☐ Confirm that all attendants know when to arrive at the rehearsal, and dinner afterward.
	☐ Confirm details with all professional services. If any changes have been made, make sure they're informed.
Two Days Before	☐ Remind your fiance to pick up his formalwear and try it on.
	☐ Make sure that the marriage license has been picked up.
One Day Before	☐ Attend Rehearsal and Dinner.
	☐ Pass out attendant's gifts if you haven't already done so.
	☐ Review any special ceremony seating arrangements with ushers.
	☐ Tell attendants to arrive at your home about one hour before you'll leave for the ceremony site if you'll be having pictures taken.
	☐ Give your fiance his gift.
	☐ Do your nails.
	☐ Get a good night's sleep.
Wedding Day	☐ Three to four hours before ceremony: Have hair done.
	☐ Apply makeup—but not with your dress on!
	☐ One and a half hours before the ceremony: begin dressing
	☐ Don't forget the groom's ring!
	☐ Arrive at the church (ask your minister/officiant, how soon you should be there). It will depend on type and location of ceremony, as well as if you'll be dressing at home or at the site.
	☐ Music should start about thirty minutes before the ceremony.
	☐ Get married and have a great day!
After the Wedding	☐ Make sure Thank You Notes are sent for wedding gifts, and for those who did special work for you. They should be sent within one month after the wedding.
	☐ Mail formal and newspaper wedding announcements.
	☐ Live happily ever after.

LAST MINUTE PLANNING

The above planning outline allows plenty of time to organize. But what if you don't have a year? Or even six months? What if you need to plan your wedding now—in just a few weeks or a month? If you have an unlimited budget, you can still have a great wedding by hiring an army of helpers—and paying huge amounts of money. If not, here are a few tips to help you manage.

It will be almost impossible to have anything other than a small, simple wedding. Limit the number of guests and attendants to fifty. Anything over that number requires more work than you probably have time to do. Remember, you don't have to justify the fact that you're getting married quickly, nor apologize for the size of your wedding to anyone.

Ask for help—your mom, maid of honor, best friends, sisters, and cousins, could all pitch in to help with making the arrangements. One might track down the reception site; another compare floral arrangements and pricing, a third organize transportation, or write out the invitations. If you don't have anyone to help you, hire a wedding consultant, or simplify the arrangements even more.

A wedding planned quickly requires flexibility in making your choices, and resourcefulness in filling your needs. You won't have much time to make decisions—but it's an exciting challenge you may enjoy conquering together.

Getting Ready for Marriage

Right now the concept of married life may seem a bit frightening. You're worried about losing your freedom and independence. You may be concerned about the responsibility involved, or the quality of your future sexual relationship. You may disagree about many things, or feel uncomfortable discussing your deepest thoughts and feelings. It's good that you're concerned. That means that you're thinking, and that you're not foolish enough to believe that love will conquer all other problems.

It takes work, communication, support, compatible goals, trust, and compromise to make a marriage succeed. And you may be surprised to find how little you really know about each other. Now is the time to discuss your ideas and expectations. It'll be a giant step towards starting your marriage off on the right track.

Married life can be quite different from the time you spend together today. The never-ending drudgery of going to work, paying bills, and doing housework will eventually rub some of the glow off of your relationship. When people live together and share both decisions and the toothpaste, little irritations can rise and compound. If not dealt with, they can brew into major problems.

Here are some questions to ask yourself and your fiance. Some are just for fun, others are about key items that could affect your future together. There are no right or wrong answers. You don't have to agree on everything—you never will. The whole point of the exercise is to start talking and thinking about these issues. To listen, understand, and respect each other's ideas and opinions. It is much better to discuss them now, than to start your marriage with too many false expectations.

How Well Do You Know Him?

Where was he born?
What was he nicknamed as a child?
What's his favorite dessert?
What's his least favorite vegetable?
What's his favorite color?
Where would he like to go on vacation?
What's the first thing he'd buy if he won a million dollars?
What's his dream car?

What Will Married Life Be Like?

How do you picture your married life together?
☐ A happy round of parties and friends.
☐ Quiet evenings at home.
☐ Family visits every weekend.
☐ Spending all our free time together.
☐ The same as it is now.
Unless you checked the last box, how do your expectations compare to your current time together? Most importantly, how closely do your fiance's expectations match your own?

Why Are You Getting Married?

☐ To spend more time together.
☐ Companionship—to avoid loneliness.
☐ To improve our relationship.
☐ To make someone happy.
☐ I can't afford to live alone.
☐ To help my career.
☐ I want children.
☐ Love.
☐ Other.

Obviously, more than one will apply. The key is to recognize your primary reasons. Are they strong enough to maintain a lasting relationship?

What Three Things Do You Consider Most Essential In A Husband?

☐ Sense of humor
☐ Financial security
☐ Respect
☐ Trustworthiness
☐ Affection
☐ Good sexual relationship
☐ Good companion
☐ Sensitivity to my moods/feelings
☐ Best friend
☐ Similar goals

How Do You See The Future?

What's the biggest adjustment you'll face after the wedding? _____
_____

List the five things you like best about your groom-to-be:
1. _____   4. _____
2. _____   5. _____
3. _____

List the five things you like least about him:
1. _____   4. _____
2. _____   5. _____
3. _____

When you think about your life together, what worries you the most? _____
_____

How do you picture your lives ten years from now? _____
_____

Having Fun

How do you like to spend your free time? _____

Do you expect him to join in or share your hobbies? _____

How much of your free time will you spend together?
          ☐ All   ☐ Most   ☐ Some   ☐ Very little

How much time can your spouse spend with friends or other interests before you consider it excessive? _____

How does your answer compare to his? _____

Will your social life be more or less active than it is now? _____

In what way? _____

How do you want to spend your vacations? _____

_____

How do these compare with his ideas? _____

How do you feel about separate vacations? _____

How important will family gatherings and outings be?
   ☐ Very important   ☐ Important to me but not him
   ☐ Somewhat important   ☐ Important to him but not me
   ☐ Not at all important   ☐ Not applicable

If your attitudes conflict, what compromise have you made? _____

_____

Finances

Do you expect to share your bank accounts, savings and investments?
_____ Payment of your debts? _____

Do you worry about his attitude toward money? _____

Have you talked about it? _____

How will the money be divided or handled? _____

_____

Which purchases will you talk about ahead of time?
☐ All
☐ Only expensive ones
☐ Only for appliances, furniture
☐ We'll each spend as we please

How does his attitude compare with yours? _____

How do you feel about credit card spending? _____

Is his attitude the same? _____

Is it important to you that bills are paid punctually? _____

Does he share the same attitude? _____

Who will make investment decisions? _____

Handle the taxes? _____

What percentage of income should be donated to charity? _____

Will you have a budget? _____

Do either of you bounce checks often? _____

Do you think it's important to save a part of your salary? _____

Does he? _____

What are your financial priorities? Do you have certain goals you're aiming

for?_____ What are they? _____

_____

Do his goals agree? _____

Do you plan to stop working if you have a child? _____

Can you live on one income? _____

Life At Home   How will household chores be divided?

Job	Him	Me
Cleaning	☐	☐
Cooking	☐	☐
Laundry	☐	☐
Shopping	☐	☐
Bill-paying	☐	☐
Errand running	☐	☐
Banking	☐	☐

Most importantly, what does he think the division of chores will be? _____

What type of meals do you like to eat? _____

How often will you eat out in restaurants? _____

Have fast food (pizza, McDonalds)? _____

Children   Do you both want children? _____

Do you agree when you'll start a family? _____

If one of you doesn't want children, can the other accept that decision? _____

What if one of you changes your mind? _____

How many children should you have? _____

Will you continue working after they're born? _____

Who will be the most responsible for their day to day care? _____

What child-rearing responsibilities is he willing to take on? _____

Would you ever consider—
☐ Adoption
☐ Abortion
☐ Artificial insemination
☐ Sterilization

How do his opinions match yours? _____

Have you discussed the use of contraception? _____

Do you agree on how and when? _____

Family Ties   How does your family feel about your groom to be? _____

Your marriage plans? _____

Do you get along with his family? _____

If either family objects to your marriage, what's their reason? _____

_____

Could it be a valid concern? _____

How do you feel about accepting financial help from family members? _____

_____

Supplying financial help to family members? _____

Do you expect to exchange visits often? _____ How often? _____

How will you spend holidays? _____

Are your family holiday practices similar to his? _____

How would you feel about your in-laws living with you? _____

Do you expect family or friends to phone ahead before they visit? _____

Future Plans

What are your three most essential future goals?

1. _____

2. _____

3. _____

Do you hope to buy a home? _____ What kind? _____

Do you hope to travel a great deal? _____

What are your career goals? _____

Do you understand, accept, and support each other's goals? _____

Whose career will have priority for transfers? _____

Will either of you further your education? _____ To what point? _____

Do you want to live in the city, country, or suburbs? _____

Will you eventually become active in civic or other organizations? _____

How do you feel about your husband pursuing such activities? _____

What's more important—a fulfilling career of a high-paying one? _____

How do you feel about putting in extra, unpaid hours to get ahead? _____

About his doing the same? _____

Traveling out of town overnight? _____

About his doing the same? _____

Have you discussed these matters? _____

How does he feel? _____

Religion

Does your future spouse share your religious beliefs? _____

If they conflict, have you discussed the matter? _____

Will you attend religious services regularly? _____

Will your spouse attend with you? _____

Will you or he become actively involved in church activities? _____

Will you observe the customs of faith in your home? _____

If it's an inter-faith marriage, how will you resolve conflicts? _____

_____

How will the children be raised? _____

Will your children be sent to church affiliated schools? _____

Do you believe in tithing? _____

Communication

Can you honestly talk to one another about your thoughts and feelings? ____

If not—why? _____

When you disagree do you—
- ☐ scream and yell
- ☐ withdraw
- ☐ not speak
- ☐ talk it out
- ☐ ignore the problem and hope it will go away

Do you feel that you should have a greater say in matters or the final word?

_____

Does he agree? _____

Do you believe he listens to you and is trying to understand you? _____

Do you do the same for him? _____

Does he agree with your analysis? _____

What subjects do you argue about the most (besides the wedding plans)? ____

_____

Do you think these problems will eventually be resolved? _____

How? _____

If not, can you live with that? _____

Sex

Are you each comfortable talking about sex? _____

Do you have the same feelings about fidelity? _____

Would you be willing to obtain help if there was a problem? _____

Do you feel that
- ☐ you're totally responsible for pleasing him.
- ☐ he's totally responsible for pleasing you.

Would you have sex if you weren't in the mood? _____

Do you expect him to have sex if he's not in the mood? _____

Do you feel that sex is proper only at a certain time or place? _____

Does he agree? _____

Do you expect your sex life to be occasionally experimental? _____

Does he? _____

Are You Ready For Marriage

What scares you the most about marriage?
- ☐ Loss of freedom
- ☐ More responsibility
- ☐ That it won't work
- ☐ Having children
- ☐ Financial problems

Do you believe that you're mature enough for marriage? _____ Is he? _____

Do you expect him to change? _____

In what way? _____

Is that realistic/probable? _____

Does he know? _____

Do you have a stable job? _____ Does he? _____

Do you make enough to live comfortably? _____

It takes work and effort to create a good marriage. You must give each other space to grow, develop interests together, and never stop listening and expressing thoughts, ideas, problems, and feelings. Resolve disagreements when you can, and try for compromise (or at least understanding) when you can't.

Don't spend too much time comparing your relationship to others. No two marriages are alike, and there are no 'rules' that will guarantee a happy life together. Every relationship has its good and bad side, and you'll never know the whole picture of anyone else's situation.

Marriage is a state of inter-dependence, not dependence. You're not losing yourself, you're adding another person to your life. You and your husband will make your own future. Your life together is an empty slate right now, it will slowly grow and evolve into one that you can live with.

I know a great book that will help you make it through the difficult adjustment period. It's called *"Newlywed: A Survival Guide to the First Years of Marriage"* (And I'm not just saying that because I wrote it). It's based on the experiences of couples who have made it. You'll find plenty of helpful advice to aid you in your new life together.

FAMILIES, FRIENDS, AND PROBLEMS

You'll quickly discover that friends and relatives each look at your wedding in a different way. Your mother might be concerned about the guest list, your father about your future finances. Your bridesmaids only seem to care about their dresses, your sister might be jealous of the attention you're getting. The only thing your grandmother seems concerned about is that she won't have to sit next to her brother whom she hasn't spoken to in twenty years.

Everyone has different ideas on what you should wear, what food should be served, where the ceremony should be held, and who should be there. You'll hear more than you'll ever want to know of any family disagreements and disasters at other people's weddings. If you invite Aunt Lucy, that means she'll bring her obnoxious new husband. However you must invite Aunt Lucy if you want to invite her sister, Aunt Kathy. Don't sit Uncle John next to cousin Fred, and whatever you do, don't forget to personally invite great-aunt Alice or she'll be insulted.

Some situations can be handled by just listening, and allowing the person their opportunity to provide input or blow off steam. Others call for important decisions—is Aunt Lucy's husband so obnoxious that you would rather limit the guest list than have him there? Then there are the bigger worries. Most families have a few members who don't get along. In some families they'll spend the day ignoring each other. In others, the angry parties might bring their dispute out in the open, with verbal and physical assaults flying around the room. Since problems usually erupt at the worst possible moment, it's best to deal with as many of them as possible in advance. That does not mean that you must resolve every family disagreement or become an expert in diplomacy.

If you know that a major problem may occur between two hot-tempered people, talk to each of them separately, before the occasion. Tell them as TACTFULLY as possible how much it would mean to you if they could make every effort to put aside their personal differences for your wedding. Ask each of them what they realistically need to stay comfortable that day. Whatever you do, don't let them drag you into their fights. Most people can tolerate a one day truce.

You, your new husband, and both sets of parents will be too busy to play the role of peacemaker at your wedding. Ask a tactful, capable person with a positive outlook on each side of the family to keep an eye open for arguments or other potential problems among people they know. You don't have to be very specific or dramatic about their role, just mention that you'd appreciate it if they'd keep their eyes open and soothe ruffled feathers if anything happens. Be sure to thank this person later.

Announcements

ENGAGEMENT

You and your parents officially announce the engagement by placing a notice in the newspaper. It should appear after you have both told closest family and friends the big news, and have set the wedding date. This allows acquaintances, schoolmates, co-workers, neighbors, and friends to read about your new relationship. Because families are so mobile today, the announcement may need to appear in several different areas. It should run in the newspaper for the towns that you and your fiance reside in, both of your hometowns, and where both sets of parents live. If there's a particular region where many friends and relatives reside, an announcement in that area's largest newspaper would also be proper.

Every newspaper has a policy about printing announcements—and some charge a small fee. The amount of information they'll include will depend on their circulation. Large, metropolitan papers have so many marriage announcements that they can only devote a small amount of space to each one. Some require a time delay between the wedding and engagement announcements. Small papers may include more details, but fewer people will read them. Check each paper's policy. The announcement might include:

- Names of the Bride and Groom.
- Your towns of residence.
- Schools attended, any degrees received.
- Both your places of employment/job titles.
- Both your parents' names.
- The date and location of the wedding.

If one of you were previously married, it's a common practice to mention that marriage to avoid confusion. For example: "(Ms. _____'s) or (Mr. _____'s) previous marriage ended in divorce."

WEDDING

There are two kinds of wedding announcements. One appears in the newspaper (similar to the engagement announcement), the other is mailed in place of a wedding invitation, and is called a formal wedding announcement.

The formal announcement is sent to those you wish you could have invited to your celebration but were unable to. They are commonly used if you've had a small wedding, but have many friends and relatives to notify. Printed or engraved on stationery similar to the wedding invitations, they are mailed immediately after your marriage (a well-organized couple has them addressed and ready to go beforehand). A person who receives an announcement isn't obligated to buy a wedding gift.

Announce your wedding in the same newspapers that described your engagement. Other information, such as details about the ceremony, wedding party, and bridal gown are usually included. It's traditional in most newspapers to print a photograph with the wedding announcement.

LIVING TOGETHER

Years ago it was considered proper to limit the celebration to a small, quiet, gathering if you had lived together before the wedding. That's not true today. Whether you shared a room for six weeks or six years, you are still entitled to all the fanfare and festivities. You will still announce the marriage in the papers, wear white, and invite your entire extended families to the party.

Money can be a sticky issue in some families. Your parents (or his) might balk at financing a wedding if you've already lived together. Your best bet is to either pay for it yourselves (more and more couples do), or see if they are willing to make a contribution and combine it with your own funds. It's also in poor taste to announce that you only want monetary gifts because you have all the furnishings you need. Most people recognize this fact on their own and will act accordingly. Bridal Registries (see that chapter) are a convenience for those guests who wish to provide merchandise.

Rings

This sentimental symbol of your commitment is not only a piece of jewelry, but a large financial investment. Take your time in making your selection. Try on different styles and shapes, and don't hesitate to shop around.

Unless he wears several other rings regularly, there shouldn't be any connection between his wish to wear one and his commitment to the marriage. Some men enjoy a wedding band, others don't like to wear jewelry. If he'll be wearing a ring, it is your responsibility to pay for it, and you'll probably want to help him with his selection. Although the plain gold band is still traditional, there are many other styles he can choose from. Matching rings are nice, but not necessary.

CHOOSING A STONE

Round

There's no rule that says you must wear a diamond engagement ring. Some brides choose a colored gemstone such as a ruby, sapphire, or emerald for the engagement. Their wedding band may be plain, or set with a diamond. Because the diamond is the most popular stone for engagement and wedding rings, most of the following information deals with selecting that gem. The cost of a stone is determined by its cut, clarity, size, quality, and color. Here's some information about each of those designations:

Brilliant

Cut: This is the stone's actual shape, the arrangement of the small surface planes and angles (called facets). The most common are illustrated here. All rough gems can't be cut into all shapes, and the artistry is entirely dependent on the cutter. In a perfectly cut stone, the facets are precisely carved for maximum beauty and sparkle. That's why some shapes are more costly than others of the same carat weight. If you find a real bargain, it probably means that it was poorly cut to maintain weight at the cost of quality.

Teardrop

Clarity: A perfect diamond will have no flaws—no specks or bubbles visible when it's examined at a magnification of ten. The fewer flaws in a stone, the more it costs, although a flawed stone can still be quite beautiful. Flawless diamonds are very rare, and very expensive. You want the fewest number of flaws for the price you can afford.

Heart

Carat: This is how the stone's weight is measured. The higher the count, the larger the stone. To compare it to a more familiar measure, 142 carats would weigh one ounce. Each carat is divided into 100 points. For example, a one half carat diamond would have a carat weight of 50 points. When it comes to gemstones, bigger isn't necessarily better. The other factors I've mentioned will influence the quality. Stones that weigh over two carats are so rare that they are very expensive.

Marquise

Oval

Color: Sometimes the sparkle of the facets can be deceiving when you are trying to determine the color of the diamond. Examine your stone under concentrated light. Cheaper diamonds have overtones of yellow, more expensive diamonds are a clear, colorless white. The most prized have a faint hint of blue.

Emerald

When picking colored gemstones they should be intense, lively, and clear (but not to the point that it appears you can see through them):

Rubies	Look for pinkish-red.
Sapphires	The best are cornflower blue.

Square

| Emeralds | Select a rich, lush green. |
| Aquamarines | Choose the very very blue. |

Quality: Although the actual terms might vary, the cut, clarity, color, and weight of each gem places it into a ratings group. Here are some popular classifications:

Royal   Superior color, exceptional clarity, superb cut. Only one stone in hundreds will meet this standard.

Classic   Good cut, quality, clarity, and color, but a slightly lesser degree of quality than the Royal. Still, a very beautiful stone.

Regal   Although it doesn't meet the strict standards of the above classifications; it can be an excellent value, especially for those who wish to have a larger stone at a reasonable price.

Radiant   If you prefer a large, but inexpensive diamond, this quality is the best. However, it doesn't meet the standards of the above three.

For the record, it's not true that only real diamonds can cut glass. Many items—including glass—can cut glass.

CHOOSING THE SETTING

When you buy a ring, you select both the gemstone and the setting (band). Your gem might be placed in a family heirloom, or in one found among the jeweler's in-stock selection. If you know exactly what you want, but are unable to find it, you can have changes made on an existing design, or have one custom-made. If you can't afford the perfect setting today, you can have the stone remounted later.

The size and shape of your hands will influence the type of setting you choose. For example, a wide, heavy band isn't suitable for tiny hands and fingers, but is perfect for larger ones. The gemstone and band should also compliment each other. A delicately cut diamond will look out of place in a chunky setting.

Bands are made of precious metals, and come in many styles from plain and smooth to intricately carved. It's customary for the bride to wear the wedding and engagement rings together, so your bands should match. Here are some details about the metals used in settings:

Gold: The amount of gold in an item is measured by karats (different from the carats used to measure gemstones). Pure gold has 24 karats, but is too soft to be used as jewelry. When mixed with other metals, it's the proportion and type of metals used that determines its value. For example, a 14 karat gold ring would be 14 parts gold, and 10 parts other metals. An item below 10 karats can't be tagged as gold in the United States. Here are some other definitions you should know:

Solid gold   Means that it's not hollow.

Gold-filled   The article contains a layer of base metal within a layer of gold.

Gold-plated   At least 1/20 of the weight of the metal in the entire piece has a plate of gold alloy not less than 10 karat.

The quality and quantity of gold in an item is usually stamped on it (except for watch cases). If you read 1/10 12k gold-filled, it simply means that 1/10 of the item's weight is of 12k gold.

Silver: Is also too soft to be used in its purest form, so it is mixed with other metals. The designation Sterling Silver refers to the composition of the metals, a combination of 92.5% pure silver and 7.5% copper.

Platinum: A shimmery, white metal that's popular because of its strength and resistance to heat and chemical damage. It's often used in the prongs that hold the gemstone to the setting.

Palladium: An inexpensive metal that weighs less than platinum, but is equally strong.

CHOOSING A JEWELER

You can purchase rings in many outlets, from Department Stores to exclusive Jewelry Shops. Remember, a 'bargain' isn't really a great deal if the stone is inferior. It's important to do business with someone reputable when buying an item that's difficult for the novice to evaluate. For your best buy, use a reliable jeweler who's a member of the American Gem Society. Ask family and friends for their recommendations. Although I've offered general information about determining the quality of an item, in the end you must rely on the integrity of the store or jeweler.

Ideally, you should have the stone examined by an independent appraiser before your purchase is completed. Choose your own. You can't discover a disreputable jeweler if you take it to the appraiser he recommended. Use a professional gemologist, a graduate of the Gemological Institute of America. Those qualifications are important. Titles such as 'certified appraiser', 'senior gemologist', or 'State/Government appraiser' may not really mean anything.

The certification you receive from the appraiser should include:

- Description by cut, style, quality, color, and carat.
- Weight
- Size
- Setting, with any special inscriptions or designs mentioned.
- Value
- Date
- Signature

Before you buy your rings, learn the store's policy about returns, refunds, exchanges, repairs, and replacements. If possible get it in writing. Any warranty should specifically indicate what it does and does not cover, and who will honor the agreement. Make sure a description of the jewelry and the material it's composed of is included on your receipt.

INSURING YOUR RINGS

Insure the rings against loss or theft. List them separately on your homeowner's or renter's policy, to make sure you'll receive full value. If you don't have your own policy, see if you can have it added to your parent's— you should pay the extra premium. The price of gemstones fluctuates, and the ring will probably increase in value over time. Have the ring re-appraised every three to five years to ensure adequate coverage.

Monetary Responsibilities

For many families it is not financially feasible for the bride's family to pay for the entire wedding. So who pays the bills? Today's couple often contributes all or a great deal toward the wedding costs. More often than not, the groom's family offers to cover some of the expenses as well. Some aunts, uncles, and grandparents offer their own financial assistance. As a starting point, here is the traditional breakdown of monetary responsibilities:

Bride:

- His ring and gift
- Her personal stationery
- Bridesmaid's luncheon

■ Bridesmaid's gifts
■ Accommodations for her attendants from out of town
■ Physical examination and medical tests

Groom:

■ Her ring and gift
■ The marriage license
■ Bride's bouquet and going away flowers
■ Corsages for both mothers
■ Boutonnieres for male members of the wedding party
■ Gifts for attendants
■ Accommodations for his attendants from out of town
■ Physical exam/medical test
■ Fee for the wedding officiant
■ The honeymoon

In *some* areas of the country, it is expected that the groom pay for:
■ Rental of gloves, ascots, and ties for his attendants
■ Alcoholic beverages on the wedding day

Bride's Parents:

■ Ceremony site rental
■ Reception site rental
■ Food/catering
■ Flowers
■ Bridesmaid's bouquets
■ Aisle carpet
■ Cake
■ Beverages
■ Decorations
■ Photographer
■ Bride's wedding day attire and trousseau
■ Musicians
■ Canopy
■ Security
■ Wedding invitations and announcements—including postage and other fees
■ Tips for bartenders, waitresses, and waiters
■ Transportation of bridal party from bride's home to ceremony and Reception
■ Their own clothes
■ Gift to the bride and groom

Groom's Parents:

■ Host the rehearsal dinner the night before the wedding
■ Their lodging and travel expenses
■ Gift to the bride and groom
■ Their own wedding clothes
■ In most cases, they're welcome to assume additional expenses if they wish to do so.

Male and Female Attendants:

■ Their wedding clothes and travel expenses
■ Their gifts to the Bride and Groom

Although a wedding funded by a combination of people allows you to have a nicer celebration, you may find yourself with too many people trying to run the show. There are three important rules to remember about wedding planning and financial contributions:

1. Paying all, or even the largest portion of the expenses does not automatically give that person total control of everything that happens that day. The things that you and your groom prefer take precedence. The bride's family are the traditional hosts of the wedding celebration, no matter how

much they contribute financially. That position of honor should not be denied them, and their input should be valued.

2. No one should be expected to give more than they can afford. If your parents can't pay for the wedding you want to have, then either pay for it yourselves or change your plans. The whole money issue should be handled with sensitivity, the poor shouldn't be shunted aside and told they have no input.

3. You owe gratitude to anyone who contributes to the wedding, and at least the courtesy of listening to their ideas. You don't have to act on them if you don't wish too, but be sure that's clearly understood if you accept their financial assistance. Don't give them the impression that you'll be doing what they suggested—then surprise them with something else. If you disagree, explain your reasons, and make sure they can accept your decisions. Take a firm stand on what's important, although it wouldn't hurt to compromise on minor points.

Budget

It's hard to determine precisely what a wedding will cost. Unless you have an unlimited budget, you'll frequently have to compromise or change the amount you'll spend before the wedding day. Start with a tentative budget, then work from there. The best way to keep costs down and have the wedding of your dreams is to shop carefully and stay organized. Compare prices and services, and deal with reputable businesses. How much will your wedding cost? Here are the percentages for a typical formal wedding:

Reception Site/Catering	33%
Rings	12%
Music	12%
Gratuities/Misc./Other	11%
Photographer	10%
Bride's Attire	9%
Flowers	6%
Invitations/Announcements	5%
Ceremony Site/Officiant Fee	2%

Set your priorities before you make a budget. What do you care about the most, and the least on your wedding day? What's your fiance's major interest? To one person, good food might be the essential concern. To another, the best music is more significant. Number the items below based on their importance to you, and have your fiance do the same.

_____ Ceremony Site	_____ Reception Site
_____ Catering	_____ Music
_____ Formal Attire	_____ Flowers
_____ Photographer	_____ Invitations
_____ Beverages	_____ Cake

Once you decide where you want to concentrate your expenditures, you can budget the rest. Consult the percentages mentioned above, so that you don't bother skimping on items that are actually a small portion of the wedding costs.

In order to stay within your budget (you don't want to be paying for your wedding for the next five years) it's a good idea to maintain records of your estimates, as well as the amount you have actually spent. The following worksheets help you by offering space for calculating three budgets, the deposits needed, and a running total of expenses. Broader categories, such as **Invitations** and **Food** are listed by section, with space to break down individual expense for each item. There's a section for *Fixed* expenses (those you have little power to change) and *Controlled* expenses (those that offer little cost-comparison, or are easily eliminated). At the end, there's an area to summarize the totals for each category.

To calculate the budget, begin by listing an *Initial Estimate* for each item. Your purpose is to determine the price range for the type of wedding you'd like to have, then compare that to the money available to pay for it. Your estimates will come from family and friends, or making preliminary phone calls. If you learn that the wedding you want will cost $5,000, but no more than $3,000 will be available, you can quickly modify your plans.

Once you've decided on the style of wedding, and researched caterers, florists, photographers, and other service providers, you can be more specific with your cost estimates. Remember that you must ask everyone the same questions to compare numbers properly. Don't price three dozen roses with one florist, and three dozen daisies at another and equate the two figures (Roses are much expensive than Daisies). Using your more detailed research, enter the amount you expect to spend for each item in the *Final Estimate* budget column.

In the example for the budget worksheets, you'll see that the *Initial* and *Final* columns list price ranges, and that your costs are still fairly flexible until this point. When you've decided the exact amount you'd like to spend on each segment of the wedding, you enter that figure in the *Target* column.

As each item is finalized—the contract is signed and deposits are made, enter the amount you paid for the item in the *Actual* column. To determine at a glance how your finances are doing, compare the *Actual* number to your *Target* figure, and enter the variance in the *Difference* column. With this method, it's easy to quickly determine if you're overspending, and by how much.

Try to allow an additional 10% in your budget for contingencies. If it turns out that the extra money wasn't needed—you'll have more available for the honeymoon! Here's an example of how to use the planning worksheets:

David and Anne are planning a formal wedding for 150 people. After their preliminary investigation, they place price ranges for their wedding invitations in the *Initial* column. After looking at several choices through various outlets, they narrow their choices to two different styles. Based on the prices of those two styles, they list that range in the *Final* column. They then *Target* the amount they expect to spend for this category in their wedding budget. When they order the invitations, they'll list the cost of the item in the *Actual* column. Since the actual cost was $10. less than their target amount, they list -$10. in the *Difference* column—they're now under budget by $10.

STATIONERY	Initial Estimate	Final Estimate	Target	Actual	Difference
Napkins, Souvenirs	25-30	35-40	40.00	41.00	+ 1.00
Announcements	20-25	35-40	35.00	23.00	– 12.00
Invitations	110-120	116-126	120.00	110.00	– 10.00
Enclosure Cards	55-60	65-78	73.00	76.00	+ 3.00
Wedding Program	30-40	25-30	25.00	23.00	– 2.00
Thank You Notes	20-25	20-23	23.00	21.00	– 2.00
Postage	80-85	85.00	85.00	84.00	– 1.00
Total	**340-385**	**381-422**	**401.00**	**378.00**	**– 23.00**

Budget Planning Worksheet

Use these planning worksheets as a **tool** to assist you in determining the kind of wedding you can afford—and as an **aid** to keep your budget on track. Although the categories that apply to weddings are covered in detail, there are blanks designated "Miscellaneous" for any additional items that relate to your situation.

STATIONERY

Deposit Required $_____ Wedding Announcements	Initial Estimate	Final Estimate	Target	Actual	Difference
Invitations					
Enclosure Cards					
Wedding Program					
Thank You Cards					
Postage					
TOTAL					

PHOTOGRAPHER

Deposit Required $_____ Engagement Photo	Initial Estimate	Final Estimate	Target	Actual	Difference
Wedding Package					
Formal Portrait					
Videotape					
Reprints					
Miscellaneous					
TOTAL					

FOOD

Deposit Required $_____ Caterer	Initial Estimate	Final Estimate	Target	Actual	Difference
Homemade					
Cake					
Miscellaneous					
TOTAL					

BEVERAGES

Deposit Required $_____ Liquor	Initial Estimate	Final Estimate	Target	Actual	Difference
Punch/Mix/Soda Pop					
Coffee, etc.					
Bartenders					
Miscellaneous					
TOTAL					

CLOTHING

Deposit Required $_____ Bride's Dress	Initial Estimate	Final Estimate	Target	Actual	Difference
Headpiece					
Groom's Attire					
Miscellaneous					
TOTAL					

FLOWERS

Deposit Required $_____ Bride's Bouquet	Initial Estimate	Final Estimate	Target	Actual	Difference
Corsages					
Boutonnieres					
Female Attendants					
Church Decor					
Trellis/Canopy					
B.V.M. (Catholic)					
Reception Decor					
Miscellaneous					
TOTAL					

RECEPTION SITE

Deposit Required $_____ Rental	Initial Estimate	Final Estimate	Target	Actual	Difference
Music					
Extras					
Decorations					
Furniture					
Set-up/Clean-up					
Miscellaneous					
TOTAL					

FIXED EXPENSES

Physical _____ Blood Test _____ Marriage License _____ Security Guards _____ Ceremony Site _____ Officiant _____
Cantor _____ Sexton _____ Organist _____ Soloist _____ Cake Delivery _____ Separator Pieces _____ Miscellaneous _____

TOTAL   Plus or Minus 10% Allowance $ _____

CONTROLLED EXPENSES

Personal: Shoes _____ Undergarments _____ Shower/Rehearsal/Going-Away Attire _____ Accessories _____ Jewelry _____
Cosmetics _____ Hairdresser _____ Misc; Lodging for out of town guests _____ In town transportation _____ Gratuities:
Ceremony _____ Reception _____ Souvenirs: Napkins _____ Ring Bearer's Pillow _____ Knife/Spatula _____
Keepsake Momento _____ Guest Book _____ Champagne Glasses _____ Gifts: Male Attendants _____ Female Attendants _____
Bride _____ Groom _____ Announcements/Newspaper fees: Wedding _____ Reception _____ Miscellaneous _____

TOTAL   Plus or Minus 10% Allowance $ _____

BUDGET SUMMARY

Deposit Required $_____ Stationery	Initial Estimate	Final Estimate	Target	Actual	Difference
Photographer					
Reception Site					
Flowers					
Food					
Beverages					
Clothing					
Fixed Expenses					
Controlled Expenses					
Miscellaneous					
TOTAL					

Your Gown

1. There may be some beautiful gowns packed away in your family's attics. Ask your mother, aunts, grandmothers, sisters, and cousins for suggestions.
2. Buy a gown off the rack in a department store. Especially if you're planning to wear a tea length dress, and aren't particularly attached to wearing white.
3. Buy a second-hand dress through a resale shop or newspaper advertisement. Think of all the beautiful gowns that were only worn once! And since there isn't a huge market for secondhand gowns, you may be able to find one at a bargain price.
4. Rent a gown. Check local outlets for details.
5. Buy the sample gown in the shop, the ones used to show different styles.
6. Ask about discontinued lines. Fashion and fabrics change each year, and many are sold at a great discount at the end of the season. A manufacturer will sometimes stop producing a beautiful dress because it's no longer profitable to make.
7. Some shops mark down their entire lines after the season. Make sure the fabric is suitable for the time of year you are marrying.
8. Several large department store chains offer wedding gowns, headpieces, attendant's dresses, and flower girl's dresses in their catalogs. The prices are very reasonable, and if you order early you can be sure to obtain everyone's proper size.
9. Sew your own dress, or have it made. There are many patterns available, or you can select a gown you love and have it reproduced in a less expensive fabric.
10. Order a bridesmaid's gown in white, use it as your wedding dress.

Headpiece

11. Once again, check the closets of family members. If the owner will allow it, the piece can be adapted or changed to match the dress. Or remove the veiling and attach it to a cap piece you've selected.
12. Buy illusion veiling material in a fabric shop and make your own. Attach it to a simple wreath or cap piece. You can decorate it with flowers, bows, lace, beads, and pearls if you like.
13. Buy a second-hand veil through a resale shop or newspaper advertisement.
14. Look for sales, discounts, closeouts, and discontinued items at bridal shops or department stores.
15. Wear flowers or a decorative comb in your hair in place of a traditional headpiece.

Accessories

16. Purchase a style of shoes that can double as dress shoes later on.
17. Buy shoes on sale.
18. Borrow shoes from a recent bride and have them dyed to match your gown (with her permission).
19. Borrow items such as the cake cutting and serving knives, wedding goblets, cake top decorations, and bridal purse.
20. Make your own bridal purse. Find a pattern for a simple drawstring bag. Purchase pretty material the same color as your dress. Stitch it together.
21. Cover elastic with satin fabric, trim with lace, and you have your own garter!
22. Make your own ring bearer's pillow.

Flowers

23. Use single flowers in bud vases as centerpieces for the reception tables.
24. Keep the number of flowers in each arrangement to a minimum.
25. You and your attendants carry a single flower.
26. If your ceremony site is not a church, have the ceremony flowers transferred to the reception site.
27. Plant and grow your own flower garden, and arrange them yourself. However, this requires a great deal of time, and shouldn't be attempted if you're having a large wedding.
28. Carry a simple nosegay in place of a large, cascading bouquet.
29. Use the most popular and inexpensive flowers of the season in your arrangements.
30. Have potted plants and flowers at the ceremony and reception sites that you can later use to decorate your home.
31. You and your attendants can carry wildflowers.
32. Buy flowers in bulk from a nursery and arrange them yourself.
33. Ask if anyone else is marrying at your site on the same day. Contact them and see if they'd like to share the costs of decorations.
34. Buy silk flowers and arrange them yourself. They can be expensive at times, so keep your eye on prices.

Invitations

35. Purchase them through mail order catalogs, often mentioned in bridal magazines. They are of good quality, and generally less expensive.
36. If you are having a small wedding, buy blank invitations (the wording is printed, with blanks for the pertinent information). You can find them at stationery or gift shops, and write them out yourself.
37. Handwrite the entire invitation on nice stationery.
38. Include the information about your reception on your ceremony invitation. This eliminates one card.
39. Send photo invitations or thank you notes. These can double as keepsake souvenirs.

Food/Beverages

40. Have a simple reception of punch and hors d'oeuvres in the afternoon.
41. Have your dinner served buffet style.
42. Eliminate the cocktail hour before dinner.
43. Use a sparkling wine instead of champagne.
44. Serve only cake and punch after the ceremony.
45. Don't provide a variety of alcoholic beverages at the reception. Limit choices to beer, wine, or punch.
46. Bake your own wedding cake. You can write to the company for directions if you use a package mix.
47. Ask a friend or relative to bake and decorate the cake.
48. Don't serve a dinner at your reception. Have it begin and end well before the dinner hour, or much later. However, your guests should be aware that they won't receive a meal.
49. Cook your own meal, and serve it buffet style.
50. Borrow items that you normally would rent, such as coffee pot, punch bowl, tables, and chairs.
51. Cook part of the meal, have the rest catered.
52. Hire your own food servers rather than using a catering service.
53. Make your guest list smaller.
54. Set your own tables.
55. Buy food and alcoholic beverages from a wholesaler.
56. Ask a friend to be bartender.
57. Buy ready-cooked food.
58. Purchase beverages from a dealer that will give refunds on unopened bottles. However, some States have laws against this.

Photographs

59. Have your bridal portrait done at home on your wedding day. (Be sure to allow enough time for this). That will save you the studio fee.
60. Rent a video camera and ask a friend to shoot some action shots.
61. Hire a professional photographer at the smallest package possible. Then offer to supply film to a few friends and ask them to take candid pictures throughout the day.
62. Ask a friend to take all the wedding pictures.

Decorations

63. Do your own decorating at the reception site. Try to get access the day before the wedding.
64. If the background site is pretty, don't bother with decorations. Once the place is packed with people, who will see them?
65. Make your own decorations. Craft books at the library will offer ideas and directions.

Honeymoon

66. Travel in off-season. Rates to popular destinations such as Florida or the Bahamas can be much lower in the summer. Find out the date the rates change and plan accordingly.
67. Camp at a State or National park near your home.
68. Instead of traveling for a week, stay one or two nights in a bridal suite.
69. If you'll be traveling by car, pack a cooler with lunch meat, soft drinks, fruit, and other picnic items. Save on lunches this way.
70. Ask about special package plans or honeymoon rates when you call.
71. Join a package tour to your honeymoon location.
72. Have a combination honeymoon; camp out some nights, stay in hotels for others.
73. If you stay in hotels, pick up a box of donuts. Eat them in your room for breakfast.
74. Check hotel regulations. Some don't mind if you bring along a hot plate. You can make tea, coffee, or soup in your room.
75. If you find yourself outpriced at your honeymoon spot, ask employees where they eat. It's often much cheaper.
76. Ask the restaurant to fill your thermos with hot coffee before you retire to your room in the evening. It will be waiting when you wake up in the morning.
77. Carry a flask of your favorite liquor. You can make yourselves pre-dinner drinks in your room.
78. Economize on meals by eating at fast food restaurants some days, then you'll have the money to splurge on a few elaborate dinners.
79. In some States, accommodations in the State Park will be less expensive than hotels and motels on the outside. Check and see if that applies to the area you're visiting. Make reservations—these places are often booked very quickly.

Transportation

80. Borrow cars from friends and family, rather than renting limousines.
81. Ask a travel agent about discounts and special plans for your honeymoon.

Men's Attire

82. Remember that proper fit of the garment can be more important than price.
83. Choose a shop that has a reputation for quality care and professional service.

Rings

84. Purchase them from a reputable wholesaler.
85. Buy at a pawn shop—but have a qualified appraiser examine them first.
86. Many coin shops deal in jewelry, and sell them for the gold content value only. That is often much cheaper.

87. Check to see if there are any family heirlooms that could be used as a setting.
88. See if divorced relatives will sell you their rings.

Music

89. Ask a friend to play the musical accompaniment.
90. Ask another friend to sing.
91. Try to bargain with the musicians, perhaps offering $50 or $100 less than their asking price.
92. Use music you taped yourself.
93. Hire a disc jockey.

Odds And Ends

94. Reserve facilities early. The least expensive places go first.
95. Hand deliver invitations to people you see often. That will save postage.
96. Reserve services early. The least expensive caterers, florists, and photographers are usually booked first.
97. Have your wedding and reception at home.
98. Reduce the size of your wedding party and you'll save on flowers, gifts, and transportation.
99. Save on lodging and transportation by asking local people to be your attendants. Out of towners can be expensive.
100. Shop around and compare prices.
101. Have a contract for every service, and READ IT CAREFULLY!

GET IT IN WRITING

No matter how friendly the salesperson, or how reputable the firm—obtain all the details in writing. It's the only way to avoid misunderstandings, or to get them easily resolved. This is essential for expensive services used for weddings, such as the caterer, musician, photographer, or florist. It'll be the only proof you'll have if things go wrong.

I'm not a lawyer, but I can offer some common sense suggestions about what your contract should include. If the firm has their own agreement, make sure it covers everything. If not, ask that the information be added, or create one yourself. The whole point of doing this is to make sure that things are spelled out—they understand exactly what you want, and you understand exactly what they'll provide, and at what cost. Never sign an agreement until everything is perfectly clear.

SAMPLE SERVICE AGREEMENT

Company Name
Address
Phone Number

Date

Your Name
Address
Phone Number

Detailed description of item or service that will be supplied...
               Size   Quantities and method of counting
               Cost   Date and Time provided
If more than one item, make sure each is listed separately.

        Person supplying service.
        Name and number to contact in emergency.
        Required amount of deposit, when balance due.
        Refund policy.
        Penalties if day is delayed or cancelled.
        Penalties if they fail to provide service as stipulated.
        Signature of service provider.
        Your signature
        Date

Your wedding will probably cost thousands of dollars. These are business transactions, and it's important to know what you'll receive for your investment. Never hesitate to question charges on a bill.

If something goes wrong, try to settle the problem by writing or talking to the person in charge. Explain exactly what the problem is, and how you want it resolved. As a last resort, you can stop payment on your check until the problem is cleared up—but that can be an expensive option. If you haven't received a satisfactory response in a reasonable amount of time, contact the Better Business Bureau, or a local Consumer Protection Agency.

Pre-Wedding Parties

After the engagement has been announced, several parties, showers, and dinners will be given in your honor. The exact number depends upon your friends and family. Here is a brief outline of the traditional ones:

ENGAGEMENT PARTY

Takes place after you've told immediate friends and family of your engagement, but before the announcement appears in the newspapers. That's usually six months to one year before the wedding date. Although the bride's parents traditionally give this party, it's becoming more and more common for the groom's parents to have one too. That way both sides of the family can meet the prospective couple. Some families throw joint celebrations and split the cost. It's usually either a cocktail party or a dinner.

Generally, you don't ask someone to the engagement party if they wouldn't be invited to the wedding. Guests don't have to bring gifts, but some might. Out of towners should be welcome, but aren't obligated to attend. However, you and your fiance are the guests of honor and must be there.

It doesn't matter if the gathering is simple or elaborate. It's just a way to officially make your intentions public, receive congratulations, and get acquainted with each other's family and friends.

SHOWERS

These affairs are hosted by close friends and family to provide you with the essentials to set up housekeeping. It's also a good way for friends, and family members to get to know one another. Although etiquette books say that it's not proper for family members to host a shower, in reality it happens all the time. Too often, family members do all the work, and put other people's names on the invitation just to display proper etiquette.

Some couples have one or two large showers, others five or six small ones. Many are theme parties, specifying gifts for the kitchen, bathroom, living room and so on. Except for immediate family, and your attendants, the same people shouldn't be invited to each shower. Remember that weddings are expensive for the bridal party too. Let them know that you don't expect a gift at each shower. In some areas it's customary, even expected, that your fiance make an appearance at the shower.

Shower invitations are generally issued to the people closest to you and your immediate family. You needn't include everyone that you invite to the wedding. Your guest list will depend on the size of each party, the number of showers given for you, and who sponsors them.

You'll also be given a personal shower by someone close to you, usually your maid of honor. At this party you receive personal items such as clothing, lingerie, and various gag gifts. This is strictly a female gathering.

It's a good idea to have one of your attendants write down the name of the giver and the gift received as you open each present. It's so easy for those little cards to get misplaced or mixed up. That can make writing Thank You notes a real nightmare! Try to respond to each gift enthusiastically. Write your notes as quickly as possible—you don't want to get backed up as the wedding gifts start arriving! See the book *"Bride's Thank You Guide: Thank You Writing Made Easy"* for hundreds of examples and ideas.

BRIDE'S LUNCHEON

This is an opportunity to gather with your attendants before the rush of the wedding day, and to thank them for their help. Traditionally it's an afternoon luncheon or tea, but you can adapt it to your own personal style—whether it's a pizza bash or a five course meal.

BACHELOR PARTY

Encourage him to have his celebration at least one week before the wedding. This trend is becoming more and more popular, because it allows plenty of time for recuperation before the big day. The party may be given by his best man, friends, relatives, or the groom himself. Generally, all male members of the wedding party are invited, along with other close friends and family. Both fathers might be asked, but generally if they attend, it's only for a short while. The style and atmosphere of the party will depend a great deal on the personality of your groom and his friends. It might range from a sedate gathering to a wild celebration. Whatever the case, you should not show up under any circumstances. That's considered very embarrassing to the groom.

REHEARSAL DINNER

Usually hosted by the groom's parents and held after the wedding rehearsal. It's style and formality depend upon budget considerations and the type of wedding you're having. It should include the wedding party, their spouses, and parents of children in the wedding. Many couples also ask their clergyman/officiant to join them at the dinner, and of course, their spouse would also be invited. It's an opportunity for an intimate gathering with those you're closest to on the night before the wedding.

Other Bride's Talk About Their Weddings

We all know that experience is the best teacher. Because a wedding is something we try to do just once in our lives, it's hard to acquire all the necessary wisdom. In this section, former brides will tell you about their own weddings—the problems they encountered, how they overcame them, and their suggestions (if they could do it again...). Although each bride has mentioned the costs of various items, you must bear in mind that you don't know what she obtained for the amount mentioned, so it will be difficult to make comparisons based on those figures alone. They are included to give you a general idea of the price ranges for these items.

Most of these women had formal church weddings, but you'll also find a home wedding, outdoor wedding, second wedding, and a justice of the peace ceremony. They paid for all or most of their wedding expenses, as has become quite customary in these days of older, more independent brides.

DEBBIE

I had an August wedding with a formal church ceremony with seven attendants. Our reception included a sit down dinner, live musicians and dancing, and over 225 guests.

After we set our date, it took us quite a while to decide on the style of wedding we wanted. At first, we thought we would prefer a quiet, simple affair. The more we talked about it, the bigger it grew. Pretty soon we just decided to have one big party and enjoy it in style.

We set a budget and worked hard to stick to it, because we paid for almost everything ourselves. We underestimated several items, and forgot to include a few others. Fortunately, we received a large number of monetary gifts so we were able to replenish the drain on our bank account!

I think my biggest problem was gathering the information I needed. I found all kinds of expensive guides to etiquette, but I needed to know how to pick a caterer or where to find a musician. I was the first one in my group of friends and in my generation to marry—so it was impossible to find any advice that wasn't at least twenty years old. That's why I'm so excited about this book—this is just what I needed. Too bad it's too late.

My two biggest mistakes were hiring the wrong people for some services—I went by word of mouth but it didn't help. The other was trying to do everything myself. This was too big of an undertaking not to delegate—but I've always had trouble doing that! Other things I regret are selecting a hall that my family had to clean up afterwards, and that I spent too much on my dress—it's only for one day! I wish I'd have spent more on my attendant's gifts to show my appreciation for all they had done.

When you're looking for a hall it's hard not to jump at the first one that looks decent that isn't booked for your date (like I did). After calling so many places that were booked a year in advance I panicked. We spent $295 to rent the hall, and that was without bartenders or cleanup. I wish I had shopped around more!

Our invitations were ordered through a mail order catalog. Their pricing was very reasonable and it was convenient to look them over at home in our spare time. They sent plenty of samples, so we had a good idea of what the quality and paper types were. Everything arrived in perfect shape, and I never had to leave my house to do anything about them. We picked invitations that included our engagement photo on the cover. I didn't order enough and had to re-order at the last minute—that was an expensive mistake. We spent about $215 on all the stationery items.

I wanted a simple wedding gown, and never planned to spend more than $150 But, I got caught up in the emotions of trying on all those beautiful gowns and before you knew it, I just had to have the one I selected. it was $685! I really overdid it. I justified it by saying my daughter or sister could wear it someday. However, it was completely ruined at the reception. Guests kept stepping on it and there were all these tears in the fabric (not at the seams). Because of all the spills, dirt, and rips, the dress is irreparable. It was beautiful, and I loved it, but it was too much to spend on something I wore once.

When I went to choose flowers I had no idea what I wanted. I was lucky because I just trusted the florist and she did a beautiful job. We spent about $400 which was in line with our budget. I didn't have many floral arrangements at the reception—once you get a crowd of people in a room who's going to notice anyway? We spent $485 for the professional photographer. I also gave one friend of mine five rolls of film to take candid shots to obtain additional records of the day. She took lots and lots of pictures, but unfortunately, she drank too much and has no idea to this day what happened to the film. The professional did a decent job—I'm glad I have those because you forget a lot as time passes and it's fun to pull them out and 'remember'. I do wish I had sat down and gone over photos with him before the wedding. Members of my husband's family kept going to him and requesting shots—so 75% of our candid photos are of his family—and they were the minority of people at the reception!

Music is important to us, so we spent a lot of time listening to different live bands. It was worth the effort because we had a great band that really set the atmosphere for a fun evening. I've heard over and over from people that they had a wonderful time dancing at our wedding. These are people who hadn't danced in years. We spent $1500.

We received a lot of conflicting advice on the amount of liquor to purchase, and ended up with a large quantity left over. Our bartenders were totally incompetent. They were free-lancers and they arrived two hours late, made the drinks too strong, and spent more time on the dance floor than behind the bar. Worst of all, we caught my uncle trying to steal a case of our liquor! The useless bartenders cost us $90 and we spent about $650 on beverages. We also had one security guard ($80). Since we had several guests who were on the local police force we felt that we had plenty of security!

The caterer, the largest bill we received, was also the biggest disaster. We spent $2380, and not all the food was served. In addition we paid for leftovers but didn't receive them. The service was poor, not all the food was cooked properly, and they seemed to have major problems doing simple things like making coffee. Ours was supposed to be a reputable company, and we had received several recommendations—but they sure disappointed us. Check references carefully—ours came from friends of friends who used them and that's too distant for a reliable picture!

Our groomsmen provided transportation for their bridesmaids throughout the day, and we were chauffeured by our best man and maid of honor. I know etiquette said we should hire a chauffeur or be alone, but I thought it would be more fun this way—and it was. After all, they're our two closest friends and it was the only chance we really had to visit without interruption that day.

My fiance and I had plenty of 'discussions' during the wedding planning. He didn't want to be bothered with all the details—yet he wanted to know why I kept going over budget. Just when I'd decide not to discuss anything more with him, he'd shock me with an interest in the tiniest details about something like the wedding invitations or the reception food. And he wasn't doing it to humor me, he had very strong opinions that didn't always match mine! He also gave me all kinds of grief over the number of bridesmaids I had selected. I have a large family and it was just impossible to eliminate anyone. He didn't feel it was necessary, but he finally dropped the matter. Whenever we had a problem, we talked it out. Sometimes we shouted and stopped speaking for a few hours, but in the end we both managed to communicate our feelings. Generally, we compromised—unless it was something too important for that like the bridesmaids. It was good practice for married life—it's full of compromises!

We're both glad we had a big wedding. You just can't replace the memories, and it's a special day. I've heard so many women who didn't have one regret it later. My biggest piece of advice to brides—and put it in giant letters—is to RELAX! Your wedding day will go by very quickly, and no matter how hard you try, a million little things will go wrong. Emotions will run high and you'll probably have a tiff or two with people you love. This is normal. Just take a deep breath and go out and have fun. I am saying this because I was a nervous wreck the whole day and let every little detail drive me up a wall. It was only later that I realized that I was the only one who even knew things had gone wrong, and that people expect them to go wrong at weddings anyway. And worst of all I had let other people's mistakes mess up my enjoyment of the day. So have fun—it's your party!

JANICE

I was married in a formal church ceremony with four attendants. We had a large reception with dinner, dancing, and 185 guests on a beautiful September day.

We decided at the beginning that we would be open to suggestions, but would only do what felt comfortable to us. Otherwise, we would end up trying to please everyone, and pleasing no one—including ourselves. We decided that the most important things to us were the band, bar, food, and cake, and that was where we would concentrate our expenditures. We didn't bother at all with souvenir items like matches and napkins with our names on them. We paid for almost everything, and we were both in school—so we just couldn't have unnecessary items!

It was very hard to plan a wedding because I was at school most of the time. I asked family members to gather information for me. I'd come home every weekend I could, and dash around visiting the places that seemed to offer the best deal. Then I'd make my decision.

If I had to do it over, I'd have kept all the details in one place. A notebook with lists of phone numbers, ideas, plans, instructions, and decisions. I'd also be more specific in assigning chores—like addressing invitations or picking up flowers. There were several mishaps due to confusion on who was supposed to do what among my bridesmaids and sisters. Next time I would even put it in writing!

Most of our time together was spent trying to find a live band that we liked. We preferred it over taped music, but it was hard to squeeze in the search in the little time we had. We spent over $1800—but we felt it was worth it. I definitely spent too much money on my dress ($400 on the dress, $100 on wreath with veil) and beverages ($580) because we had plenty left over. We cut corners on the photographer ($390) and I wish we hadn't. We seriously considered videotaping but just couldn't swing it financially. I wish now we had.

We disagreed about the number of bridesmaids, I wanted six and he insisted on four. That and the style of invitations turned into major problems between us. In the end I gave in on both counts. It just wasn't as important to me as it was to him—although I still don't know why he cared so much.

He was from Minnesota, I was from Indiana, and we were both going to school in Illinois. So, we had groomsmen spread across three States which turned into a real problem. Men aren't very motivated when it comes to weddings, and we had a heck of a time nagging everyone to get measured. My husband's roommate never did bother—and in the wedding pictures he's wearing pants about 8 inches too long. It looks terrible and it makes me angry that he cared so little about how he would look.

I couldn't decide what I wanted in flowers, so I bought silk ones since they last forever. I kept the arrangements very simple—each of my bridesmaids carried one white rose and wore a floral wreath. I'm glad I chose silk, I still have my flowers and everything looked very nice. I spent about $285. A private party made the cake that cost $220, plus $25 refundable deposit for the decorations. We had two security guards at the reception and paid them $70 each. We used the caterer that came with the reception hall. They served a basic menu, and the food was delicious. Total cost for hall and caterer was about $2100.

Tell other brides to start early, and plan and organize everything. Also, I can tell them a few things that I've had happen at other weddings I attended that made me very unhappy as a guest. I went to one where they wrote their own ceremony; it lasted over an hour and it was really boring. Don't make yours too lengthy. The worst reception I ever went to they spent too much time taking pictures which delayed the dinner by two hours. We were starving! There didn't seem to be any direction of what to expect the whole evening. No announcements or introductions. People just milled about. To top it off they had a cash bar—which I think is tacky beyond belief. One other thing. Please send Thank You notes for your gifts. We've attended several weddings where we gave gifts and never received acknowledgement. That really hurt. It cost us money to buy a gift, get dressed up, have my hair done, and drive there, and time—which is pretty valuable to us. The least they could have done was shown some appreciation for our effort!

SUSAN

We had a very small church ceremony in December. There were just two attendants, and afterward we went to a restaurant for dinner with immediate family. There were about 20 people.

Most of my time before the wedding was taken up by nerves! I had a hard time deciding about my dress, my flowers, and my attendants. I was really worried about how I'd look. I needed to be reassured over and over that everything was okay. You see, we met, decided to get married and took the big step in just three months. We both had second thoughts and lots of nervous attacks in the final days. Maybe it was best we did it so fast—less time to think about it!

Our biggest worry was money—and that was the groom's biggest concern. He didn't care how I did anything, but he cared about the cost. We would just sit down and talk things out, and usually found a way to do what was important to us. If I could do it again though, I'd like to have a big, beautiful wedding and reception. With mountains of flowers, a long line of bridesmaids, limousines, a band, the whole works! But, I wouldn't go in debt to do that.

My dress was the easiest to choose because I fell in love with it the minute I tried it on. It was a satin and lace gown for $375. which was way over budget, especially for one day. But, I felt beautiful in it, and that's important too! Flowers were another matter. I was really disappointed and thought the arrangements were much too thin for the price I paid. We spent $175. for artificial flowers. We gave the minister $180 which was more than we expected but we didn't belong to that church. Be sure to check beforehand and confirm he has the correct time and date. We almost had a real mix-up and no minister, but things were straightened out in time.

Tell other brides that it doesn't hurt to listen to advice, but you have to make your own decisions. Don't let anyone tell you what to have, it's your wedding. And organize yourself early. You'll be so glad you did. I'd also say that you shouldn't do anything you can't afford, you don't want to be paying for your wedding a year later. There are too many other things that can happen and if you start out behind you'll never catch up. I would also suggest from my own experience that you should choose attendants clothes at a price range they can afford. At a friend's wedding the money box was stolen—so keep it well away from the door and hire good security. Most of all, don't panic! Just have fun.

MARY

We had a formal wedding in church, with a dinner reception for 100 guests. I had four attendants, and married in early March. It took us a long time to decide on the size of our wedding reception, and the hardest decision we faced was selecting the reception site. I made it a point to shop around and not just buy the first thing that I saw. I also relied on friends and relatives for helpful advice.

There are two things I'd change if I could do it again. I wouldn't have gotten married in winter. We had a snowstorm the morning of the wedding, and my mom's phone rang constantly with people calling and saying they couldn't make it. Fortunately, it cleared up by the time of our ceremony, and had melted by the reception. The other problem happened before the wedding, and it was with the bridal shop I used. I was originally supposed to get married in January, but had delayed my wedding date. When I contacted the shop they told me that was no problem, they'd just hold the bridesmaid's dresses for my new date. When we went in a few weeks before the wedding to pick them up, they had sold them all to someone else without notifying us! Not only that, they refused to return our deposits. The woman denied talking to me, and claimed no one picked up the dresses within thirty days so they had a right to sell them. I tried for several days to resolve the issue, but just didn't have the time or energy for such a major battle. My fiance and I reimbursed the bridesmaids for the money they'd lost, we felt it was only fair. My bridesmaids swore they'd do more damage to that shop by word of mouth than anything they gained by selling our gowns, and I hope they have. Luckily, my sister had gotten married the year before and we were able to borrow the bridesmaid's dresses from her wedding.

We had an embarrassing moment at the reception. We had decided that my brother-in-law (who was the Best Man) should say grace at the reception. Unfortunately, I thought my husband had talked to him about it. About two minutes before dinner started, I said something about saying grace. He refused. We endured several agonizing minutes while we argued with him, then asked a few others who said no because they were too shy. Meanwhile, the guests sat there and stared trying to figure out what was happening. Finally, my grandfather said yes and he said a beautiful prayer. Tell other brides to cover every detail themselves—you can't be sure it's done unless you do it!

That was the biggest problem I had with my groom. He wanted me to make all the arrangements, and he would just show up. We sat down and talked about it, and I thought we had worked it out. He says he just forgot, but it sure made me mad!

We didn't have music at the wedding, and now I wish we'd have hired a band or a disk jockey. My dress and hat were $355, and most everything was about what we expected it to be. We spent $170 on the cake, $160 on invitations, $350 on photographer, and about $200 for silk flowers. The minister just asked for a donation, we gave $85.

Remember when you are comparing services that salespeople can be helpful, but they're trying to sell you something. If you have your mind set on an item, stick to it. Ask around about different businesses such as bridal shops before going there. You don't want to get burned like we did! And try to include him, no matter how much he objects. I think *The Groom to Groom Book* will be a big help for getting men involved in the planning and preparation. After all, it's his wedding day too!

NANCY

We wrote our own ceremony which took place in June at a non-denominational church. We dressed formally, had four attendants, and a reception for 125 guests that included a sit-down dinner and taped music for dancing.

I had difficulty finding sources of information to make my decisions. I spent so much time gathering details, trying to find the best for each price that we ran out of time. By then, I was so tired of it all that I just randomly picked places, and things, and ended up going way over budget.

You might hear that silk flowers are less expensive, but that's not always true. We had budgeted $150 for flowers, but somehow the bill for my silk flowers was $345! I wish that I had shopped around, and had a better idea of what I wanted and needed before I ordered them.

We had budgeted $180 for invitations, but were able to save money in that category. We spent $150 for 200 invitations, and all the stationery that you buy with them. Be sure to order extra, it's cheaper and there will always be forgotten people, requests for souvenirs, or mini-disasters like spilling coffee on a few when you're addressing them. Our cake was also within budget at $155.

Our biggest mess was with the photographer. My two sisters had used the same studio for their weddings and they did a beautiful job. For my wedding that photographer sent his new assistant, who just did a terrible job. His pictures didn't look that good, and it all ended up costing a lot more than we thought. We budgeted $350 and spent $585—and they weren't willing to give us any kind of break on the bad job done by the new assistant. When you pay so much money you expect the best so it was pretty frustrating. My advice to other brides is to shop around, and be sure to find out which photographer will take your wedding pictures. Look at samples of ones they've taken, and be sure to see if they charge extra for taking pictures at the house, outdoors, or after a certain time at the reception (mine did).

When you choose your attendants, I think it's a good idea to stick to family, or very close long-time friends. Others just aren't as committed to helping you, and you don't know how close you'll be when the wedding rolls around. You should also let them choose their attire—and it should be something they can afford. It's not fair to wipe out their budgets for your wedding!

As you look at reception sites, note the differences in what they offer for their price. Some offer catering, bartenders, and liquor with no extra charge for the hall. Others, you rent the hall and hire all the services yourself. Be sure to ask about decorations, and don't forget security. Try to use off-duty policemen. In most places, private security guards don't have legal authority to stop and detain anyone. You also need to arrange for a guest book stand, gift and cake tables, and a microphone for the best man.

We liked having taped music for our wedding. You can hire a service, or do it yourself. A friend of ours used his time and equipment to make our tapes as his wedding gift to us. We borrowed albums and tapes from everyone we knew. It took time to organize it all, and decide which songs to use and what order to put them in. Cassettes were easy to work with, you just make them up for each part of the day (receiving line, dinner, dancing, etc.) Be sure to allow for last minute changes!

If your groomsmen will be chauffeuring for the day, remember that if they have a small car it's harder for the bridesmaids to get in and out with long gowns. And don't forget to arrange for backups, in case of car trouble. Go over meeting places and times at the rehearsal. If you do it too much sooner, things might be forgotten. Have maps ready if necessary.

Advice for other brides:

1. Don't spend time worrying about what other people think. Listen to suggestions, but do what makes you happiest and forget about the rest.
2. Before you begin your planning, decide together how much the groom will contribute to the process, then go your separate ways. If you nag him after that, he's going to react negatively. Remember that he's nervous too—whether he'll admit it or not.
3. Most people don't know the difference between a $200 dress and an $2000 dress. Don't let emotions overcome common sense when it comes to your selection. Stick with what you can afford. If you look good in it, that's all that's important and there are plenty of attractive, inexpensive dresses.
4. You should realize right now that you'll probably blow your budget, you're going to make mistakes, you can't please everyone, and people will disappoint you. If you accept that these things will happen, it'll be easier for you.
5. Allow plenty of time for planning, and don't be afraid to have help. Line up people for everything from addressing invitations to having someone run for ice at the reception if necessary.
6. Your wedding will be a hectic, emotional day. Every bride cries at least once. Give yourself ten minutes of quiet relaxation at some point between the wedding and reception to be all alone, by yourself, so you'll have time to regroup.
7. It's your day, don't let anyone ruin it. Whether it's Aunt Sally's comments, or the groom's drinking at the reception.
8. Keep smiling!

MELANIE

We had a quiet July wedding at my parents home. A family friend who's a judge performed the ceremony, and my husband's best friend played the guitar and sang a few songs. We each had one attendant, and after the ceremony we had a buffet-style dinner. Most of the food was made by me, my mom, and my grandmother.

I wore a simple, long white dress and the groom wore a suit. Our total cost of clothing was under $200. We had about fifty guests which was too large a crowd for the house. Fortunately, many people went outside because the weather was so beautiful. The total cost for food was $180, and liquor and beverages were under $80. A friend made the cake and charged us $50, and another friend took pictures as his wedding gift to us. Our only other expense was the flowers, they came to $60.

We had a small wedding to save money. I regret not being able to have more people at my wedding. I also underestimated the amount of work involved beforehand. For two weeks before the wedding we worked day and night, cleaning, painting, and cooking to have everything looking great. I was exhausted on my wedding day!

The biggest problem I had was that my groom wanted to elope. Even this simple wedding was too elaborate for him! He considered this a giant compromise—and so did I since I always wanted a big wedding. If I could do it again, I'd have written our own ceremony, and had a big reception with a hall and dancing. One nice thing about a wedding like ours is that you don't have the potential for major problems—there isn't much that can go wrong when you keep it this simple.

My advice to other brides is to enjoy your wedding—no matter what. It doesn't matter if it's not the day you'd dreamed of, or if things don't go exactly as you planned. It all passes too fast to waste time wishing things were different. It's your special day, have a great one.

DONNA

We married in my husband's church and had five attendants. It was a formal wedding, held in May. Our reception included a sit-down dinner, live band with dancing, and over 345 guests. I'm so glad that we had a church wedding instead of going to a justice of the peace like my friends kept telling us to do.

Organization is the biggest part of planning a wedding. We reserved our reception hall and band over a year in advance. I had a lot of trouble finding out what I needed to know, and making all the decisions.

If I could do it again, I would have shopped around more, and saved more money ahead of time. I'd also have spent more money on our wedding rings and the invitations. We had silk flowers, and my mother made all the arrangements. It came to $130, less than we budgeted. The hall supplied their own decorations so we didn't need many flowers there. My uncle took the pictures as his wedding gift to us and that saved quite a bit. And a private party made our cake for $185. We sent out 360 invitations; I think we spent about $245 on those. And it seems like most of my time was spent writing and sending out the invitations. We spent too much money on food, the caterer was very vague about many of the expenses. They did a reasonable job but we didn't appreciate the damage to our budget. We spent a lot of time worrying about what the bill would be on our wedding day.

We were lucky to receive 95% of the money we spent on the wedding back in monetary gifts. But, we were burned by the caterer—both by the size of the bill and the fact that the leftover food that we paid for was stolen by the waitresses. Tell other brides to shop around before making choices!

You should also send out your invitations in plenty of time, to give your guests a chance to arrange their schedules. People are so busy these days they need time to plan things.

ELIZABETH

We had a formal church wedding in November with five attendants. Our day included a large reception with dinner, dancing, and 350 guests.

I was very organized and planned every detail. I read everything I could find, asked a lot of questions, and started planning more than a year before the date. We wanted a particular hall, and chose our date for the earliest time we could get it. Everything went pretty well, and if I could do it again I wouldn't change a thing.

The hardest part was helping my groom understand the planning. He was from a Southern family, and I'm a Midwestern Polish girl. He was used to a simple wedding ceremony, with a reception of cake and punch, then everyone goes home. I wanted a big, Polish wedding, and that's what we had. To top it off, he lived out of state while I was doing most of the planning. I'd describe things that I'd done, and I think he walked around shocked by the scope of it all. The number of guests, the big showers, the mountains of food, the partying—all that goes with an ethnic wedding. In the end, he had a great time, but still looks back at it as quite an involved ordeal.

Our biggest, and most time-consuming problem was with family members. We had so many people pushing their ideas on us—it wasn't easy to stick to what we wanted. We just did the best we could and things seemed to work themselves out in time. Listening to different bands and musicians took a lot of our time. Fortunately we found a wonderful group that was well worth the $2350 we paid them.

I decided to try to save money where I could, but I made sure I had what I wanted—even if I occasionally went over budget. Our hall didn't charge for rental because we used their caterer, and the charge was $13.75 per person. We had about 350 people there, so that was our biggest expense. They raised the price from what they had quoted us, but it was in their contract that they could do that so we had to pay. Our cake was $240 and made by a private party. I think our flowers were about $695—and they were beautiful. However, I'd advise taking a color chart with you so that you leave nothing to chance. My interpretation of the color mauve was quite different from the florists! Our invitations were $370, and we gave the priest a $100 donation. Although we spent more than we budgeted for the photographer, I think it was well worth it for all the beautiful memories those pictures evoke. We paid him $885, and treasure every photo. The only problem we had was that he moved out of state before the wedding. He flew in for it, and we handled proofs through the mail. I also went way over budget on my dress and hat, I spent $1150. I gave them a picture of the hat I wanted, and they adapted one to my wishes.

I'd tell other brides to personally check all details, and check references before you sign a contract. Most importantly, this is an emotional time and you are bound to have problems with the different expectations of your parents or other family members.

LISA

We married by the side of a lake on a sunny August day. We had six attendants each, a buffet style dinner with an outdoor reception. There were about 250 guests at our party. We dressed formally for the ceremony, but everyone brought casual clothes for the reception. There was swimming, volleyball, softball, and lots of music.

We went way over budget, although we didn't have to pay for the site because my grandfather owned the land the lake was on. My uncle made us an eight tier cake for $245; my flowers were beautiful but cost $480, and the pictures were well worth the price of $650. We spent about $225 on invitations and $600 on liquor/beverages. Our music was from tapes that we made ourselves. Family members made all the food, cost of groceries was about $1100. My dress and veil came to $580, and I wish I hadn't spent so much now.

The hardest decision for me was to choose who to have in the wedding party, between friends and members of the groom's family. He and I argued a lot during the planning, about things I never thought he'd care about like the cost of my dress and the color the bridesmaids wore.

I'm so glad we married outdoors. The weather was beautiful and the pictures turned out great. However, if you're planning an outdoor wedding be sure to have an alternate site in case of bad weather. I was a nervous wreck because it poured for three weekends before our big day—so I prayed a lot!

As for problems with the wedding itself—four people were stung by bees, and police came because of complaints that the music was too loud. It was echoing off the lake. I'd inform other brides to try to work with their fiance to work out agreements. I think in our case we did so much fighting and had so many worries I'd rather have eloped.

CATHY

We had an evening semi-formal church ceremony, with one attendant each, and a very small gathering of just thirty people afterward. Our reception was a family style dinner at a restaurant and a two-tiered cake for dessert.

This was my second wedding, and I had a difficult time finding information to help me make decisions. I either received outdated advice, or just 'do your own thing' attitudes. I wanted to have something nice, to make the day special, but also keep it very simple.

I had problems finding a dress in a suitable style and the right material for January. I couldn't decide what color to wear, and finally selected off-white. My gown was floor length with a jacket, styled along the lines of an evening gown.

Although I felt uncomfortable inviting anyone since my first wedding had been a large celebration just a few years before, it was also hard to limit the guest list. Because the groom had brothers and sisters and I didn't, I decided to include my aunts and a cousin I'm close to as my guests. I told everyone not to give gifts but they did anyway.

My most complicated problem was finding a church. My first marriage was in the Catholic church, and because I hadn't received an annulment yet I couldn't marry there. It was important and meaningful to me to have a church wedding, but I didn't know where to go. It seemed like every place I called wanted us to join their congregation. They made me feel I had to justify remaining Catholic because I couldn't be married in that church. I just kept calling around until I found a minister that would marry us without insisting we convert. He did a beautiful job too; it was a lovely ceremony.

Because everything was small and simple, I don't remember what I paid for anything. I remember the flowers were quite expensive, and didn't stay fresh very long. It was hard to find invitations I liked, and it took forever to write them all out!

Our big disagreements were all centered on the fact that he wanted to elope. So any discussion about the wedding, guest list, or related plans always wound around to his feelings that it was unnecessary. We talked it over, and once he realized how important it was to me, he left the matter alone.

If I could do it again, I'd turn back the clock and erase my first marriage. Then I'd have a big Catholic wedding with lots of people, and a big reception with dinner and dancing.

As you plan, don't be afraid to ask for advice or to follow it. Keep the groom up to date on your ideas and arrangements. And I think silk flowers are your best choice because they stay nice forever so you get more for your money.

DIANE

Our wedding took place in the office of the local justice of the peace, with just the best man and maid of honor present. We dressed in semi-formal style, and had a simple reception with fifty guests that included a buffet dinner but no music.

We wanted a big wedding with a band and everything but just couldn't save enough money. His family was used to large weddings and expected one, where mine had always felt cake, punch, and just immediate family present was enough. So ours was a compromise. Since no one we knew had planned a wedding like ours, it was difficult to get advice. In the end, we paid for everything ourselves (except the liquor) and did the best we could.

My wedding was an awkward situation from beginning to end. To begin with, I was pregnant and we were both seniors in high school. We told our parents in December and they were very upset. My father refused to allow any kind of Christmas celebration in our house, no tree or gifts which made my little brothers and sisters resent me even more. We graduated mid-term in January and married in February. The problem wasn't just our age. We came from different religious faiths, and both families strongly objected to our marrying outside the faith we were raised in. In fact, the justice of the peace ceremony was our solution to that tug of war. Both sets of parents refused to attend.

To top it off, my family doesn't approve of alcoholic beverages, my husband's family thinks that they're part of a celebration. So his father supplied and paid for them. Because we agreed to that, my parents refused to pay for any part of the wedding, so we had to come up with the money for the rest. At our reception, his mother wore black. My parents came, but refused to allow my brothers and sisters because I was now considered a bad influence on them.

We tried compromises, and I feel we did the best we could under the circumstances. There was no way around our problems because we were dealing with so many narrow minds. What helped us was other family members on both sides...aunts, uncles, and cousins were very helpful and supportive. We still have hard feelings about the whole situation; it took a long time before we could be nice to each other's parents.

What we never understood is that since we loved each other and wanted our baby, what else could we do? I know we're young, but why give us so much grief? It wasn't great that I got pregnant in high school, but it happened and we were trying to make the best of it.

I wore a formal wedding dress that I rented, and he wore a suit. We didn't have many flowers; I think we spent about $75. A friend made the cake and charged us $60 for materials. My cousin took the pictures, and she and other relatives pooled their snapshots and presented us with an album as part of their gift to us. Our biggest and most expensive mistake was the food. We bought way too much, spent about $280, and had a lot of leftovers.

If I could do it again, I'd have saved more money to have a big church wedding. I don't think there would have been a way to avoid all the problems with our families, and we probably compromised too much. We tried to make everyone happy and in the end no one was satisfied. Tell other brides not to let emotions cloud their thinking. If your feelings are hurt, it's hard to listen to advice, no matter how practical it sounds. And remember, it's your wedding, so try to make yourselves happy.

Disasters and Mishaps

You've probably heard a few stories about unusual incidents at the weddings of friends or family. Things go wrong at weddings, there's no way around it. To give you an idea of the things that can happen, I've compiled a list of those that the bridal advisors have heard about. Don't let it discourage you, most of these 'mishaps' only contributed to the fun of the affair. Remember, guests are there to have a good time and will adapt themselves to most situations. In fact, in many cases the guests at these weddings weren't aware of the problem unless they were told.

...My ex-boyfriend came to my wedding, started a fight with one of my friends, and put him in the hospital. I wish I'd have had him thrown out immediately after he came. I had security but didn't think to use it!

...Our best man was driving us around after the ceremony and the muffler fell off his car. It was a new car too.

...My cousin's wedding veil was accidentally set on fire by someone's lighted cigarette. They put it out quickly but her veil was ruined, and she was a bit shook up.

...My uncle was caught stealing liquor at our wedding.

...Just before we left for the reception site it was decided that we wouldn't have enough mix for drinks. Two groomsmen were dispatched on that errand. Meanwhile, we all went on to the hall. We left the two bridesmaids they were escorting for the day at my mom's house, the men were supposed to swing by and pick them up. They forgot. So did we. The bridesmaids had a hard time finding a number for the hall, then getting anyone who answered to help them. Finally, they sent someone to tell us the problem, and the groomsmen dashed off to pick them up—an hour after the reception had started.

...I was a bridesmaid in a wedding where my escort's car broke down. We had to get a rental car.

...In our church, it's a tradition to kneel and say a few prayers at Mary's shrine before the ceremony begins. Until that moment I was calm, but suddenly my knees started shaking so badly that I couldn't stand up. The priest kept motioning for me to rejoin the groom. The soloist kept singing the last verse over and over. I could feel everyone's eyes on me, and I was terrified that if I tried to stand up I'd fall over. Finally, my matron of honor physically pulled me up and took me to the altar. And I was positive I wouldn't be nervous!

...No one checked to see if the bride's train was completely in the car. It dragged along the ground the entire five mile ride to the church, and was ruined before the day even started.

...We used my husband's company car on our wedding day. The attendant's decorated it with shaving cream and the paint job was completely ruined. It left permanent marks of the words in the paint.

...Even though we had a signed contract, the band never showed up. Finally, my brother went home and got his tape player and tape collection to save the day.

...Someone wrote 'help' on the bottom of the groom's shoes, and when he knelt down at the altar...

...While the photographer was taking a picture of our rings, we suddenly realized that my wedding band didn't match my engagement ring. What made it worse was that we moved out of state immediately after the wedding, so I had to exchange it by mail.

...Shortly after our reception started the lights went out, and there was no way to get them going again. The band couldn't play, there were no pictures, and the ice melted. All that money...the hall had a clause in their contract that protected them in disasters such as that.

...I was at a wedding where the groom and the bride's brother got into a fistfight.

...The bride and groom drove themselves to the reception. Their car broke down out in the country, and they had to walk three miles down that country road in their wedding attire!

...Near the end of our reception I realized that I had lost my birth control pills. We were flying to the Bahamas the next morning. After some frantic telephoning, we found an all-night drug store forty miles away. My brother went and picked them up.

. . . The bride insisted that her entire list of pictures be taken after the ceremony, even though it delayed the start of the reception by almost two hours. The guests were starving and frustrated, the smart ones ran to a local fast food outlet.

. . . We went to a wedding where the bride was so hung over from the night before she barely stumbled down the aisle.

. . . When I threw my bouquet two of my cousins scratched and fought over it.

. . . The groom's sister's car was vandalized during the wedding.

. . . I know a bride who missed her rehearsal dinner because she was still making the bouquets.

. . . Someone spilled a whole bottle of champagne on the bride's dress at the reception.

. . . The bride tripped on her wedding train.

. . . We forgot to take the guest book to the reception.

. . . It was so hot in the church that the bride fainted.

. . . One of my bridesmaids drank too much, and spent the whole day wildly flirting with the husbands and boyfriends of the others. Since she was my husband's cousin I didn't know her very well. But, I spent the whole day listening to fighting and tears from all of them.

. . . Our bartenders drank too much, and spent more time on the dance floor than at the bar.

. . . My bustle snaps and hooks weren't sewn on properly and we couldn't bustle my train. People kept stepping on it, and my dress was torn in so many little places. It was totally ruined.

. . . The worst wedding I ever went to the bride and groom ignored everyone and had a cash bar.

. . . We paid for our own wedding, and the groom forgot the checkbook. Since he lived an hour away from the reception site, and it snowed heavily that day, the best man spent a good part of the day going back to the groom's apartment to retrieve it. We asked the caterer if they could wait, but they insisted they had to have a check that night.

. . . When the groom picked up his tux the night before the wedding, he discovered he'd been given the pants of a man four inches taller and thirty pounds heavier than he was

Making Basic Decisions

Wedding Styles

This chart details the four basic types of weddings. Styles will overlap because of local customs, ethnic heritage, and personal preference. Generally, the more formal your wedding—the closer it should follow traditional social etiquette.

	Very Formal	Formal	Semi-Formal	Informal
Style	Traditional, elaborate, costly	More relaxed, most popular	Flexible-between formal and informal	Catch-all, anything that you want.
Ceremony	Church, Synagogue Temple, Ballroom	Church, Synagogue Temple, Ballroom Home, Country Club	Anywhere Proper	Anywhere Appropriate
Reception	Large, lavish dinner and music	Stately dinner and music	Usually includes meal, maybe music	Small and simple repast.
Guest List	Over 200 guests	Over 100 guests	Usually less than 100	Seldom more than 50
Bride	Elegant long dress, long sleeves/gloves long train, veil	Long dress, any sleeve length, veil, shorter train	Morning wedding-knee length. Evening-floor length, veil/hat/wreath	Dress or suit with hat, or casual clothing
Males	See charts in "Male Attire" chapter for complete details.			
Female Attendants	6 - 8 attendants Long dress, gloves headpiece	2 - 6 attendants Long dress, headpiece	1- 3 attendants Based on length, style of bride	One Attendant. Dress or suit or casual if approp.

MILITARY WEDDING

If you or your fiance are officers in the United States Military (regular or reserve) there are options that can enhance the style of your wedding. (Although an enlisted man or woman can marry in uniform, the remainder of the celebration would follow civilian traditions). Begin by talking to your commanding officer about local protocol and traditions. Here are the general customs for military weddings:

Guest List

If your groom lives at the military post, you should invite all officers and their wives to the ceremony and reception. If your fiance lives off base, you can just invite your commanding officer, post commander, and their wives.

Clothing

You can wear your uniform, but most women opt for the traditional gown.

Ceremony Site

You can marry at the chapel on base, at a church, or at a site of your choice off base. An American flag and the standards of your military unit are usually displayed during the ceremony.

Ceremony Seating

Rank should be carefully observed when seating guests. High ranking officers should receive seats of honor.

Ceremony

Because officers traditionally wear their swords on the left side; a bride stands to the right of her groom. (In a civilian wedding, she stands at his left). All ushers, whether civilian or military, stand to the left side of the bridesmaids in the processional.

Arch of the Swords/Sabers

This epitomizes the traditional military wedding. After the ceremony, the ushers either precede you and your groom down the aisle in the recessional, or leave by a side entrance. Outside the church, officers in military dress form an arch with their swords or sabers (Army) with the cutting edge facing up. You and your groom pause under the arch, kiss, then walk through. It's traditional for the two end guards to use their sabers or swords to tap the bride and groom on their backsides as a sign of good luck.

Civilian attendants do not take part in this ceremony, although they may line up with the officers. Enlisted personnel in the wedding party would stand at attention. If your entire wedding party is composed of civilians and/or enlisted personnel, it's possible to arrange for an honor guard to perform this task at some bases.

Wedding Cake

If your groom is in uniform, it's customary for him to cut the wedding cake with his sword or saber.

Second Marriage

This will be a special celebration of new hope, with a unique, wiser understanding of the commitment involved. Years ago, it was considered proper to have a very small wedding ceremony and reception if the bride or groom had been married before. Today, anything goes—especially if neither of you had a formal wedding the first time, or if one of you were never married.

If you or your groom have children, make sure they are the first to hear the news, and that it comes from you. Reassure them that the new spouse is not trying to replace the other parent. Give them an opportunity to express and discuss their feelings. You should each set aside time to provide emotional support in the week before the wedding. Ask your former spouse to help shape the children's attitudes by exhibiting a positive outlook toward your new marriage.

Try to involve them in the ceremony, but don't force the issue. They may serve as honor attendants, readers, acolytes, candle lighters, guest book handlers, punch servers, flower girls, or ring bearers. If nothing else, have them escorted to their seats of honor near the front. Ask a friend or relative to keep an eye on them during the day, and offer extra assurance when necessary. It's important that the children feel loved, and that they are a significant part of the occasion. Give each child a special gift to commemorate the day. Even if they don't appreciate it now, they will later. Try to keep the honeymoon short if the children are young. This marriage is a dramatic change and they need the reassurance of your presence. You may also have them join you for the latter part of the trip.

Every religious denomination allows for remarriage in certain situations. It's up to you to discover if your circumstances meet church policy. It might mean obtaining a church decree or annulment—or pre-marital counseling. Here are the basic positions of some of the larger denominations:

Assemblies of God, Baptist, Lutheran, Methodist, Presbyterian, Reform Jewish: Depending on the number of prior marriages and your relationship with the church, most local ministers/rabbis will agree to perform a marriage after some counseling.

Catholic, Eastern Orthodox, Episcopal, Mormon Temple Marriages, Orthodox and Conservative Jewish: Members must obtain a church decree, divorce, or annulment; and some require a letter from the Bishop sanctioning the new marriage.

Feel free to wear what you like. There's nothing wrong with a white floor length bridal gown with all the trimmings. (Although most second-time brides don't use a face veil). The groom and the rest of the wedding party will base their attire on your style of clothing. Most couples marrying for the second time host and pay for their own celebration. As part of that independence, they often walk up the aisle together.

Guests who gave a gift at the first wedding are not obligated to give another, but many will. You can spread the word, and even note it on the invitation if you prefer not to receive a gift. Or just invite them to a party— and surprise them with a wedding!

Types of Ceremonies

CIVIL

Performed by a judge or authorized officiant, it may take place anywhere, from the judge's chambers to your backyard. Usually this is a small, informal wedding, especially if both parties have been married before.

RELIGIOUS

Personal preference, and the religious beliefs of you and your fiance will determine the type of wedding ceremony you'll have. If you share similar religious backgrounds and beliefs, it will be an easy decision. If you are of different denominations, you may agree on one ceremony, try to combine ideas from both, or write your own. The important thing is that you discuss the matter, and that you both feel comfortable with the final results.

In this section I've provided some information about marriage ceremonies of the major religious denominations. It will help you learn about different churches, especially if you are undecided about which to choose. If you're writing your own ceremony you may find it interesting to read about the rituals of different faiths. Or if you are marrying in an unfamiliar church (your fiance's) it will help prepare you for what to expect. There are so many options and practices in every religious denomination it is impossible to offer more than basic data here. Consider it a starting point for your discussions with the minister, priest, or rabbi.

ROMAN CATHOLIC

Marriage is considered to be a lifelong commitment in the Catholic Church, and is one of their seven sacraments. Because of this, almost every parish requires the couple to participate in pre-marital counseling in order to prepare for their new roles and responsibilities. It is generally advised to contact the parish priest at least six months before the wedding date. Most Catholics wed in the bride's church, but it's not a requirement. It is customary for banns (the names of the bride and groom and their intention to wed) to be announced for three consecutive Sundays preceding the marriage in the parish bulletins of both the bride and groom.

Any Catholic who has been divorced must have a church sanctioned annulment. Some divorced non-Catholics might also have to obtain an annulment before marrying in the Church.

If you request an inter-faith ceremony (a special dispensation from the Bishop is needed) the church tries to consider the faith of a non-Catholic by allowing his or her minister to participate in the ceremony. Unless additional dispensation is obtained, this wedding would not include a Nuptial Mass.

The church prefers that all Catholic couples marry in a Nuptial Mass because of the importance this celebration brings to the occasion. If your ceremony will be part of a Nuptial Mass, it will take place in a church. Home or garden weddings usually need special approval from the Bishop of the diocese. Weddings are discouraged during Advent, Lent, after 6 p.m. on Saturday, or on Sunday. Any exceptions must receive special dispensation. Although the Church prefers that the two witnesses for the ceremony be Catholic, it's not a requirement.

You can usually choose from a selection of readings, prayers, and hymns for your ceremony. Vows cannot be changed from the traditional words of the church. Some priests will permit the addition of appropriate phrases if they do not change the meaning of what's being expressed, or violate the beliefs of the church. It's still traditional in many churches for the bride to make a brief visit to Mary's shrine to place flowers and ask for her prayers. Many grooms are now visiting the shrine of St. Joseph at the same time. This can occur after the bride is escorted up the aisle, or prior to the recessional.

Catholic brides are not 'given away', they are escorted to the altar. Your escort can be your father or anyone close to you, both your parents, or even both sets of parents if you like the idea.

The Mass begins with an opening prayer, shortly followed by readings from the Bible. Those selections are often read by a friend selected by the couple. The priest or deacon then reads from the New Testament, and may give a short homily. When it is time to recite the vows he will say:

My dear friends, you have come together in this church so that the Lord may seal and strengthen your love in the presence of the church's minister, and this community. In this way you will be strengthened to keep mutual and lasting faith with each other and to carry out other duties of the marriage. And so, in the presence of the church, I ask you to state your intentions.

_____ and _____, have you come together freely and without reservation to give yourselves to each other in marriage? Will you honor each other as man and wife for the rest of your lives? Will you accept children lovingly from God, and bring them up according to the laws of Christ and his church? {Couple answers}

Since it is your intention to enter into marriage, join your right hands and declare your consent before God and His church. {The groom, then bride each repeat the vows}

I, _____, take you, _____, to be my (wife) (husband). I promise to be true to you in good times and in bad, in sickness and in health. I will love you and honor you all the days of my life.

OR

I, _____, take you, _____, to be my (wife) (husband), to have and to hold, from this day forward, for better, for worse, for richer, for poorer, in sickness and in health, until death do us part.

The priest now says: You have declared your consent before the church. May the Lord in his goodness strengthen your consent, and fill you both with his blessings. What God has joined, men must not divide.

He blesses the rings, the groom places the ring on the bride's finger and says:

_____, take this ring as a sign of my love and fidelity. In the name of the Father, and of the Son, and of the Holy Spirit. {In a double ring ceremony, the bride would do and say the same to the Groom}.

The Mass continues with the Prayer of the Faithful, Liturgy of the Eucharist, Nuptial Blessing, Sign of Peace, and Communion. Non-Catholic guests should not partake of Communion in a Catholic church, because the Catholic belief in the Eucharist is much different than that of other faiths. A final prayer and blessing would complete the service. (If there is no Mass, only the prayer and blessing would take place after the ring ceremony.)

EASTERN ORTHODOX

Although they share similar beliefs and ceremonies with the Roman Catholic church, they do not acknowledge the Pope as their spiritual leader. Inter-faith marriages are allowed if the non-Orthodox person is a baptized Christian. A religious decree of annulment is required for divorced persons. Weddings are not allowed during certain holy days or seasons of fasting.

The traditional Orthodox ceremony takes place in the afternoon or evening, and no Mass is celebrated with the wedding ceremony. The bride and groom will fast, make confession, and take communion before the wedding. The ceremony takes place in front of the sanctuary. A nearby table holds a Bible, cross, chalice of wine, candles, and flowers.

The repetition of three, representing the Trinity, has great significance in the Eastern Orthodox church. The betrothal ritual begins when the priest blesses the rings three times at the altar. In a double ring ceremony, he then places each ring first on the groom's finger, then on the bride's. The best man then exchanges the rings three times on the fingers of the bride and groom. As part of the ritual the priest places a gold-plated crown on each head (or white wreaths made of imitation lemon flowers) to symbolize a victorious marriage in a world full of evil. The crowns are exchanged between the couple's heads three times.

After a New Testament Reading, the couple drinks from the same glass and wine three times to signify their willingness to share everything in marriage. Just before the final vows are made, the priest will bind together the couple's hands, and lead them (along with the other members of the wedding party) around the table three times. The congregation sings: *"God Grant Them Many Years"* during this part of the ritual, which reminds the couple that love and marriage never ends, like an unbroken circle. Throughout the ceremony the bride and groom hold lighted candles, symbolizing the light of the Lord.

PROTESTANT

There are so many different denominations that it's difficult to discuss available options because each sect has their own practices and traditions. Some churches allow you to write your own service, others allow you to select among pre-approved options. Discuss church regulations and practices with the clergy member you have selected.

Restrictions vary: Some won't hold weddings on Sundays or holy days, others may have objections to candles, photography, or certain music. Some require additional paperwork if one of you has been divorced. In most sects, inter-faith marriages are accepted as long as one partner is a baptized member of that church. Some churches will ask for a church judgement before approving a marriage of a divorced person. Many will require a few pre-marital counseling sessions with the minister, and ask that you attend their services.

Many wedding ceremonies are based on the Book Of Common Prayer. After welcoming the assembly and making a short statement about the purpose and institution of marriage, the minister says:

"Dearly beloved, we are gathered together in the sight of God . . ."

The couple are asked their intentions, and to show that they understand and accept the responsibilities of marriage.

Who gives this woman to be married to this man?" The bride's father, brother, or whoever escorted her down the aisle responds "I do" or "Her mother and I do".

Selections from the scriptures, usually chosen by the couple, are read. Some churches allow a more secular ceremony, with poetry, songs, and other writings used in addition to or in place of the Biblical readings. Sometimes the bride and/or groom give a short talk about their feelings and emotions for each other. The readings are followed by a communion service (optional).

The minister will talk about the new roles taken on by the couple, the traditional speech being:

"Marriage is an institution ordained of God, blessed by Jesus, established and sanctified for the happiness and welfare of man, into which spiritual and physical union of one man and one woman enter. Cherishing each other's infirmities and weaknesses, comforting each other

45

in times of trouble, providing honesty and industry for each other and for their household, praying for each other and living together the length of their days as heirs of grace . . ."

The pledges are now recited, the traditional being:

"I, _____, take you, _____, to be my wedded (wife) (husband), to have and to hold from this day forward, for better, for worse, for richer, for poorer, in sickness and in health, to love and to cherish, till death us do part, according to God's holy ordinance; thereto I plight thee my troth."

The rings are blessed and given to the couple to exchange. The groom places the ring on the bride's finger, saying "With this ring I thee wed . . .", and the bride places the ring on his finger repeating the same vow.

After saying a prayer for the new couple, the minister pronounces:

"Forasmuch as _____ and _____ have consented together in holy wedlock and have witnessed the same before God and this company, and thereto have pledged their faith to each other, and have declared the same by joining hands and by giving and receiving rings, I pronounce that they are husband and wife together, in the name of the Father, and the Son, and the Holy Spirit. Those whom God hath joined together let no man put asunder. Amen."

The ceremony often ends with the entire congregation reciting the Lord's Prayer.

JEWISH

The three interpretations of Jewish traditions in the United States are Orthodox, Reform, and Conservative. Your ceremony will depend on which interpretation you and your fiance follow.

Orthodox is the strictest adherent to the Holy Book and Jewish law. The wedding ring is always of plain gold. Because custom decrees that the ring is the groom's gift, some rabbis will not allow a double-ring ceremony. No inter-faith marriages are allowed, and the rabbi will not marry divorced persons unless both religious and civil decrees are obtained. All weddings take place in the synagogue, where the bride and her family are seated on the right side of the church, the groom and his family on the left (opposite of Christian tradition). In Orthodox churches men and women sit in separate areas of the synagogue, and the service is in Hebrew and Aramaic. Before the service, the bride and her attendants receive guests in an ante-room. The couple stands under a chuppah or canopy before the Holy Ark (which corresponds to the altar in Christian churches). Both sets of parents stand with them during the ceremony. The ring is placed on the index finger of the bride's right hand during the ceremony. She can move it to her left hand after the ceremony if she wishes.

Conservative tradition falls between the strictness of the Orthodox and the progressiveness of Reform. All marriages are held in the synagogue, and the rabbi will not officiate a marriage of mixed faiths. Before the ceremony, the bride is seated in an anteroom with her attendants and receives guests. The service is in Hebrew and Aramaic. Men and married women cover their heads, and the bride and her family are seated on the right side of the church, the groom and his family on the left (opposite of Christian tradition). The couple stands under a chuppah or canopy before the Holy Ark (which corresponds to the altar in Christian churches). Both sets of parents stand with them during the ceremony. The ring is placed on the index finger of the bride's right hand during the ceremony. She can move it to her left hand after the ceremony if she wishes.

Reform interprets Jewish law in a much more liberal and progressive manner. A chuppah (canopy) is not required, nor do the parents stand with the couple during the ceremony. Inter-faith marriages, as well as ceremonies outside of the synagogue are possible with some rabbis. In most ceremonies some customs and traditions of other Jewish sects are observed (such as seating) but others are not (the bride's ring is placed on her left hand). The Reform service is usually in Hebrew and English.

The Jewish wedding ceremony can take place at any time except: the Sabbath, a regular fast day, the festivals, the three weeks from the seventeenth of Tammuz through Tisha b'Av, or during the thirty-three day period of Sefira. Any number of attendants are allowed, and parents and grandparents often participate. Most couples wed beneath a chuppah (canopy) which symbolizes the home. If the chuppah is large enough, the two principal attendants and the parents will stand with the rabbi and the couple underneath it. All ceremonies must have at least two male witnesses.

A small covered table containing two cups of ritual wine and one glass wrapped in a white napkin are next to the Rabbi. The groom is required to provide the bride with a gift—usually the ring suffices.

The ceremony begins with a prayer, followed by the betrothal blessings. After the first blessing, the rabbi passes one glass of wine to the groom, who takes a sip and gives it to the bride. The ring ceremony now takes place. In some States, if the ceremony is in Hebrew and Aramaic, the rabbi is required to say in English, "Dost thou take this (man) (woman) to be thy wedded (husband) (wife)?' The usual response (I do, I will) must also be made in English. The marriage contract (ketuba) which obligates the husband to support the wife is read aloud, then signed by the couple.

After a short talk to the new couple, the rabbi recites or chants the seven blessings (there must be ten males [minyan] present to do this). Then the bride and groom seal their pact by drinking the second glass of wine. The groom crushes the wrapped glass beneath his foot. That tradition is to remind all present that Jerusalem was once crushed. Even in this happy time they must remember their obligation to rebuild Zion.

CHURCH OF JESUS CHRIST OF LATTER DAY SAINTS (MORMON)

Members of this church can be married for 'time' or for 'eternity'. Marriages for eternity are performed in the temple after the couple has undergone extensive counseling. Church officials must approve their temple marriage before it can take place. When the couple are pronounced man and wife, the priest declares them wed for time and all eternity (instead of "till death do you part"). Children of this marriage are believed to belong to the couple in the eternal world.

Couples married for time (till death) can obtain a civil marriage from the bishop of the church, or any accredited officiant. They can later remarry in the temple if they meet the requirements for church approval.

INTER-FAITH MARRIAGES

Members of two similar Protestant sects would only have slight adjustments to make. A marriage between a Christian and a Buddhist would require tremendous adaptation on both sides. The policy on inter-faith marriages varies among the denominations. Some, such as Orthodox Jews, will not allow them under any circumstances. Most base their decision on individual circumstances. A dispensation from the Bishop is required in Catholic churches, but it is difficult to find a rabbi who will agree to participate in such weddings. Churches that allow inter-faith ceremonies will often co-operate by allowing both ministers to take part, and to incorporate the traditions of both faiths in the service.

The location of the marriage will depend on the denominations involved. Most rabbis object to ceremonies held in a Christian church, and it's not necessary for Jewish ceremonies to take place in the synagogue. Some Catholic diocese do not allow outdoor or home weddings. Sometimes a neutral spot, such as a hotel reception room, inter-faith chapel, or outdoor garden is the best solution.

Be sure to have the clergy communicate with one another early in the process. Usually the clergyperson of the institution where the wedding is to be celebrated will lead the planning process. Almost any priest, minister, or rabbi that agrees to officiate an inter-faith marriage will want to discuss your future plans—which church will you worship at, how will children be raised? For most, their main consideration is not whether you belong to their church, but making sure that you've thought about possible future conflicts.

NON-DENOMINATIONAL CEREMONIES

If you would like a church wedding, but do not agree with the religious beliefs of a specific sect, you may choose to select a non-denominational church (such as the Unitarians) for your ceremony. Instead of creeds or laws, this church has a philosophy of spiritual belief. Your ceremony can reflect whatever doctrine and personal religious feelings you wish to express. You can write your own, or ask the minister for suggestions.

Personalizing Your Ceremony

If you want to add a personal, creative touch to your wedding, you can write your own vows, change the words of traditional vows, or make other adjustments to a ceremony. However, some churches won't allow changes, and others limit your options to pre-approved selections. Be sure to talk to your officiant before you take the time and trouble of writing your own ceremony.

The first rule is to keep both speaking parts to a minimum, especially if you plan to memorize it. Whatever the case, have a typed copy handy at the ceremony. Even if you feel calm through all of the preparations and before the ceremony, more than one bride (and groom) has had knees, stomach, and memory turn to jelly once the ceremony began. The emotions and excitement of the moment should never be underestimated.

A ceremony usually begins with a greeting to the guests, a mention of the purpose and meaning of the gathering, and often includes a request for the prayers of the congregation. Readings from the Bible or other writings may follow. The officiant may then give a short talk about marriage—it's meaning, responsibilities, obligations, challenges, and benefits. This talk might include a description of a good marriage, and advice to the couple for attaining that bond. Or, if you prefer, you and your groom might choose to talk about your love for one another, and marriage and it's meaning to you.

Before the actual vows, the officiant usually describes their purpose and meaning. Then each of you say, read, or repeat your vows, answering "I Do" or "I Will" at the appropriate time. If you wish, another prayer, blessing, or reading can follow your pledges.

Before the rings are exchanged, the officiant will ask for God's blessing on the rings, their wearers, and this marriage (if it is a religious ceremony). You may instead select a song or reading that will introduce the symbolism of this portion of the ritual. Then you exchange rings, saying, reading, or repeating a sentence to mark their significance.

After the ring ceremony, the officiant will pronounce you husband and wife, citing his authority to do so (invested in me by this State). At that point, the congregation might be asked to join in a prayer for the new couple, or asked to applaud them.

Read through the vows described in the Religious Ceremonies section; and check your library for books that will help you with your own. You may wish to include personal rituals. One that is popular today is the lighting of a unity candle. During the ceremony two lit candles stand on either side of a larger unlit one. After the ceremony is completed, the bride and groom each use one of the burning candles to light the center one together, symbolizing their new unity.

You might have a favorite song played or sung during your processional, or other meaningful music throughout the ceremony. Add to the traditional ritual by composing your own prayer, or speaking a few lines about your personal feelings for each other and your new commitment. Have the ushers hand a single rose to each guest as they arrive. As you move up the aisle, stop and take a single rose from your bouquet and hand it to your mother. Then cross the aisle and do the same for his mother. Ask to have the church bells rung after you say your vows.

The most common sources for wedding ceremonies include: The Bible (especially the Song of Songs), writings from *The Prophet* by Kahlil Gibran, the poem "How Do I Love Thee?" by Elizabeth Barret Browning, "Sonnet Number 116" by William Shakespeare, and "There is a Place Where Love Begins" by Carl Sandburg. Additional sources include: lyrics from songs incorporated into the vows, and of course your own creations.

Give a typed copy to the officiant at least a week before the ceremony so he can familiarize himself with it. Be sure to provide proper directions: Do you wish to face the congregation or the altar during your vows? Should he read the vows and have you repeat them, will you memorize them, or do you want to read them to each other? Even if you don't plan to memorize your part, read through your ceremony several times so that you will feel comfortable reciting the lines.

Selecting the Ceremony Site

Your ceremony site is not only the place where you exchange your vows, but also a part of your wedding celebration. No matter where it takes place, it should be a location acceptable to both of you. Here are some points to consider when making your decision:

CHURCH/TEMPLE/ SYNAGOGUE

Most weddings take place in a house of worship. If you don't belong to the same religious denomination, choose the one you both feel most comfortable with. If neither of you have such ties, but would like a church wedding, attend services together. If you find a place that you like, talk to the clergyman. Policies for marrying non-members will vary from place to place. Some require that you attend religious instruction classes or marital counseling sessions first. Others have no such restrictions. If you can't agree on religious beliefs, consider a non-denominational church (such as Unitarian) for your ceremony.

If you are of the same religious faith, it's customary to wed in your church. Or you might select your college chapel, an outdoor shrine, the groom's church, or a location that has a special meaning behind it for your ceremony.

Here are a few practical details to consider when making your decision:
☐ Is it large enough for the number of guests?
☐ Could it be too large?
☐ Does it have an organ?
☐ Is there enough parking available?
☐ Will they schedule other services the same day?
☐ If so, what amount of time will be allotted for your wedding?
☐ Is there adequate temperature control/ventilation?
☐ Is there a place for you (and a separate one for your groom) to wait before the ceremony begins?
☐ Are rest rooms available?
☐ If it rains after the ceremony, is there a place to greet guests indoors?
☐ Is there a charge to use the site?
☐ If you're not a member, will you be charged an extra fee?

HOME WEDDING CEREMONY

This has both sentimental and economical advantages. Traditionally, your parent's home is used, although yours, the groom's, his parents, or that of a close friend or relative would work. In most cases, the number of guests is quite limited, depending on the size of the home and availability of parking.

Before you choose this option, consider the amount of decorating, painting, cleaning, and yard work that will be involved. If major renovations are necessary to prepare for the wedding, it may not be as cost-effective as you think. Don't forget to unplug the phone and put away the pets. You don't want any jarring interruptions in the middle of the ceremony!

OUTDOOR CEREMONY

A wedding at a lovely park, on a stunning beach, in the mountains, or among landscaped grounds is always romantic. When you marry in public, try to pick a location away from popular attractions, unless you don't mind strangers at your ceremony. If possible, spend a day at your site to thoroughly familiarize yourself with the daily traffic. As with any location, you must consider parking and other facilities, and be sure to arrange for someone to clean up after the ceremony.

Where will you stand? Will the sun be in your eyes at that time of the day? Remember, outdoor weddings take place in a natural environment. That might mean a ceremony with pesky dogs, wild bees, persistent insects, rain, blazing sun, wind, snow, sleet, or hail.

HOTEL/CLUB/ RESTAURANT WEDDINGS

Shop around for the atmosphere, room size, and price range that suits you best. There's often no charge for site rental if the establishment caters the wedding—although that option isn't always as cost-effective as it sounds. This is a great idea if you'd like the ceremony and reception to be held in the same place.

CITY HALL/ JUSTICE OF THE PEACE

Make an appointment to discuss details and fees. This type of wedding is always informal, flowers and other extras are kept to a minimum. However, don't hesitate to ask a friend to come and photograph the moment—it's still a special celebration no matter how simple or small it is.

ALTERNATIVE OPTIONS

Arrange to be married at a local historic mansion, famous garden, art gallery, or historical site. Some couples wed on rented yachts, others in private rail cars. Perhaps the spot where he proposed, or a place special to the two of you would be best. The options are as wide as your imaginations if you want something 'different' for your ceremony.

When families are scattered across the country, some couples are reviving the old-fashioned ethnic tradition of multi-day celebrations. The family gathers for a long weekend of parties and activities—the wedding and reception are just part of the fun. Other couples take their wedding on the road, visiting family and friends around the country, with parties and celebrations at each stop.

CHOOSING THE OFFICIANT

Meet with the officiant to discuss the type of ceremony you prefer. You want it to be significant to both of you. Although many details are regulated by religious denominations, there are usually a number of options to choose from. Ask for a copy of the traditional ceremony, and what choices are allowed. Don't be afraid to ask for advice. He or she will be experienced in these matters.

Ask what fees are involved—and for suggestions on what to pay the sexton, organist, cantor, etc. This is usually a touchy area, and many clergyman don't like the payment to be called a fee, preferring the term donation. This is because many turn their income from weddings back to the church. Others refer to it as an honorarium. The cost can vary, depending on the church, it's popularity, and the status of your membership. Plan from $75 to $800.

If you're marrying in a house of worship, you may have to provide records of church membership (such as baptismal/confirmation certificates). If it's not your home church, you may have to provide a letter stating that you are a member of good standing in your own church.

A civil ceremony can be performed by a judge, justice of the peace, or captain of a ship. It can be as short or formal as you like. If you want an elaborate ceremony, or one that takes place outside of the officiant's office, be sure to make prior arrangements.

Selecting the Reception Site

The traditional wedding reception takes place in the evening, and includes both music and a sit-down dinner. However, here are a few other options to consider:

Breakfast   If you marry early in the morning, you might have a breakfast gathering at a local restaurant. You can have the wedding cake for dessert. Alcoholic beverages are unnecessary this early in the day.

Lunch   This would take place between 12 and 2 p.m. Have either a buffet style or sit down meal with cocktails. Serve wedding cake for dessert.

Tea   Usually held between 2 p.m. and 5 p.m., you would serve only coffee, tea, or punch. Hors d'oeuvres are available for snacking, and the climax of the party is the cutting of the cake.

Cocktail   Starts between 4 p.m. and 6 p.m. and is similar to a tea reception. The difference? It just starts later, and alcoholic beverages are served. There's usually an open bar for the guests.

Dinner   Usually starts between 6 p.m. and 8 p.m., and a cocktail hour may precede the dinner. Guests are served a full meal—it doesn't matter if it's sit down or buffet style. Alcoholic beverages are available (unless it violates strong personal beliefs). The cake is cut and served after dinner, or wrapped in napkins for the guests to take home.

CHOOSING THE SITE

Your reception is the celebration of your new marriage. Once you determine the size of your guest list, the amount of money you can spend, and the style of the party; you must choose a location. Here are some ideas:

Church Halls

Many churches have halls that they rent out for weddings. You don't necessarily have to be a member of that denomination. However, if you will have alcoholic beverages at your reception, check their policy. Some churches won't allow it on their premises.

Fraternal Organizations

Many fraternal organizations rent their halls to non-members. Try the Moose, Elk, Knights of Columbus, Eagles, Fraternal Order of Police and Veterans of Foreign Wars lodges in your area. (You'll find them in the phone book). Each have their own rules and regulations.

Restaurant/Banquet Room

Check under those listings in the phone book, or visit restaurants and ask about their facilities. Be sure to see the room. Is the atmosphere and size suitable for your celebration? If it's a small wedding, ask if you'll have a separate room. Some places might just block off a corner of the public dining room for your reception.

HotelCountry Club Ballrooms	Visit sizable hotels and ask to see their facilities. Some country clubs will rent to non-members. It doesn't hurt to ask.
Park Pavillion	City, County, and State parks may have suitable rooms for rental in their park pavilions.
Home	Make sure there's enough room for everyone to move about comfortably, and that plenty of parking is available. It's best to offer a buffet style meal. If it will be on paper plates, make sure they are sturdy. Non-messy foods are your best choice.

Outdoor

Provide a canopy over both the eating area and bandstand in case of sudden storms. If the reception will be held after dark, be sure that plenty of lighting is available. As you consider your options, here are some questions to ask:

☐ Is it available for your date?
☐ Is it large enough for your number of guests?
☐ What's the rental cost?
☐ Amount of deposit required?
☐ When is the balance due?
☐ Does the room have separate heating/air conditioning controls?
☐ Can you adjust them, or will someone be available to alter them on your wedding night?
☐ Are enough restroom facilities available?
☐ Do they decorate for the wedding?
☐ Do they provide catering? Cost?
☐ Are you required to use their caterers?
☐ Are there enough tables and chairs available?
☐ Who sets them up?
☐ Are enough dishes, flatware, etc. available?
☐ Do they provide microphones? Guest Book stand?
☐ Do they have bartenders? Cost?
☐ Must you use them?
☐ What's their liquor policy?
☐ Must you use their house liquor?
☐ Do they provide security? Cost?
☐ Are they insured for accident or theft?
☐ Who's responsible for cleaning?
☐ What time will the doors be open for guests—or be accessible to you if you must decorate?
☐ What time must the hall be vacated?
☐ Is there a penalty fee if it hasn't been vacated at that time?
☐ What's the name and number of the person you can reach on your wedding night in case of emergency?

Be sure to have a written agreement for this arrangement, and verify it a few weeks before the wedding.

Wedding Customs—Where Do They Come From?

Your wedding will honor traditions that are based on some very old customs and superstitions. Practices that originated to ward off evil or bring good luck are now followed because it's the accepted way of doing things. I thought you might like to learn a little about the history and background of some customs and traditions—starting with the act of getting married.

Marriage

We've all seen cartoons of a caveman slugging his intended bride with a club and dragging her off to his cave. It really might have begun that way. A capture or kidnapping of the bride before the wedding ceremony was a custom that continued until recently in some parts of the world. It was a ritual—with envoys, decoys, and negotiations. In fact, the origin of the wedding party and the honeymoon evolved from this custom.

As time passed, men began to purchase a bride. Wives were valuable property because they held three jobs—wife, housekeeper, and childbearer. A man's purchase price also reassured the bride's father that he could afford to take care of her.

Later, the concept of the bride offering a dowry to be married offered a new twist to the negotiations. The man was still expected to provide a gift of value, but a dowry gave the bride a bit more independence. Now she brought something of her own to the marriage—besides her ability to fulfill the womanly tasks expected of her. She was no longer beholden to her husband for everything they owned. Because the dowry remained in the husband's control only for as long as the marriage stayed intact, it also offered her security against divorce.

As property holdings became more complicated, and dynasties were established, arranged marriages became commonplace. Young children were often betrothed in order to provide security for their families. The betrothal itself was very serious, with contracts and rituals to mark the step. If either party died, or backed out of the arrangement, the other could lay claim to half their property.

Rings

Tokens or symbols of marriage have always been customary. In ancient cultures, only married couples were allowed to hold hands. Sometimes the bride and groom tied weeds around their wrists as proof of their bond. For many years, a gold coin was broken in half at the ceremony, for each to carry as a symbol of their relationship. Eventually, the more noticeable symbol of a ring gained widespread use, perhaps based on the Egyptian view that the ring, an endless circle, was a sign of unity and continuity. The ancient belief that the vein from the third finger ran directly to the heart made that location popular for rings.

Rings with gemstones became available to the average person after nineteenth century exploitation of the African diamond mines. This custom quickly became popular, and remains so today. Although the wedding band is often plain, it's traditional for the bride's engagement ring to sport a gemstone.

Wedding Party

The custom of having attendants began when men captured their brides. The groom would enlist the aid of his friends to help with the abduction. The bride was surrounded by maids to protect and comfort her. The best man would serve as a decoy, to distract the bride's protectors while the groom and his other friends swooped in. After the kidnapping, the best man served as negotiator to re-establish relations between the families.

Later, the superstition developed that a couple were especially susceptible to evil spirits on their wedding day. Female friends of the bride dressed identically with her, and the groom's friends dressed exactly as he did. The practice was believed to fool the spirits as to who the real bridal couple were. Neither the bride or groom were ever left alone; each was constantly escorted by two members of their sex in the wedding party.

The wedding party took on more duties over time. In ancient Rome, they participated in ceremonial functions and protected the couple's money and belongings throughout the festivities.

Wedding Showers

These probably originated during the time men bought their brides. To enable a poor man to marry the woman of his dreams, friends would get together and present him with gifts that he could use to buy her.

Flowers

The bride and her maids once carried bouquets of strong smelling herbs (such as chives or garlic) to ward off evil spirits. Later, sweet smelling flowers became popular, and certain ones were felt to have symbolic meanings. Even today, the lily represents purity, a rose means beauty, orange blossoms represent fertility, and ivy is meant for good luck.

Bride's Dress and Veil

White became the popular color for wedding gowns in the fifteenth century. It was believed to symbolize the woman's purity, and help her to ward off evil spirits. Until then, women married in their best dress, or national costume.

The practice of wearing a wedding veil evolved from a different custom. Although women usually wore hats to complete their wedding outfit, many believed that a veil covering the woman's head would help the bride ward off evil. In addition, since most marriages were arranged without either bride or groom meeting before the ceremony, a veil over the bride's face would remain in place until the vows were finished. Then the groom would lift the veil to view her for the first time.

In the Near East, the bride and groom were carefully separated by a curtain throughout the ceremony, under the belief that bad things would happen if either of them saw the other before the wedding ceremony.

Rice and Roses

Where did today's practice of tossing rice or rose petals at the couple originate? The Greeks and Romans of ancient time threw kernels of wheat and corn at newly married couples. Indians threw rice. They did this to wish the couple luck and prosperity. They used grains because they represented food and fertile regeneration, and the couple were wished plenty of both.

Food and Cake

Sharing food and cake has been part of wedding celebrations since they began. Communal eating has always been a way to reaffirm binding ties. In many early societies, the sharing of food and drink together was the entire wedding ceremony. Even in early Rome, a couple wasn't considered legally wed until they ate bread together.

Today, sharing wine and bread (or communion wafers) is still a part of many Christian ceremonies. Jewish and Japanese ceremonies also include a ritual of drinking wine together.

Celebrations

Music and dancing have followed dining at wedding celebrations since earliest times. They originally called on the gods to bless the celebration or were meant to drive away demons. Today, they're a way for everyone to participate and have fun at the reception.

The custom of the bride and groom having the first dance symbolizes their place of honor at the festivities. Or it might have evolved from puritanical European traditions. Back then, the couple was expected to dance the first three dances together. Everyone watched them closely to decide if any premature lovemaking had taken place.

If you think your reception lasts too long, be glad you didn't marry in nineteenth century Wales. The custom there had guests drinking, singing, and toasting the new couple outside their bedchamber for about a week.

Toasts

This tradition began in sixteenth century France. At that time, lavish feasts were very popular. A man would drink to the health of one of the ladies. A piece of bread was then placed in the bottom of the goblet of wine, and the cup passed to each guest. The honored lady would be the last to receive it. She would eat the wine-soaked toast and receive everyone's compliments.

Clinking glasses during a toast comes from the early belief that the best way to chase off evil spirits was to make bell-like noises.

Breaking the wine glasses was a tradition that signified the glass wasn't worthy of being used again for any reason. Shattering items was also believed to ward off evil spirits in many peasant communities. These practices are not that popular today.

Tossing the Garter

It's customary at most weddings for the groom to remove the bride's garter and toss it to a waiting group of unmarried males. This tradition evolved from an old British custom called *flinging the stocking*. After the bride and groom had retired to their bedchamber, the guests would burst in and grab their stockings. Then each would take turns sitting on the edge of the couple's bed and flinging the stockings at the couple's heads. If anyone had theirs land on the nose of the bride or groom, it was believed they'd be the next to marry.

Tossing the Bouquet

The bride was considered lucky. Guests would rip off a piece of her gown to have a portion of that good fortune. To spare their attire bride's began to sew ribbons on their gowns to be torn. Eventually it evolved that the only lucky person would be the one who caught the bride's bouquet.

Honking Horns

Making noise after the ceremony is finished—whether it's honking, trumpeting, clattering, setting off firecrackers, or shooting guns into the air—are traditions around the world. It began as another way to frighten off evil spirits. Today it's a method of announcing that the event has taken place.

Honeymoon

In the days when the groom captured his bride, the couple hid from her parents for one month, or until the moon waned. By tradition, the search was dropped at that time. While they hid, they drank honeyed wine to sweeten their bond. Just like couples today, it was a time to get to know each other better and begin their relationship away from the pressures of work, family, and friends.

Carrying Her Over the Threshold

Another custom that comes from the kidnapping days. This was done to get her into the house without allowing her an opportunity to run away.

Good Luck Charms

If you are superstitious, here are some traditional portents of good luck for your marriage:

1. Your engagement ring has his birthstone in it.
2. Members of the wedding party are already married.
3. Wear a coin in your shoe during the ceremony to ensure future wealth.
4. Keep a fragment of the wedding cake to be sure of his lifelong fidelity.
5. Wear something blue during the ceremony to signify your fidelity.

Bad Luck Portents

Here are the things you should avoid if you're superstitious:

1. If the engagement ring is lost, the marriage will suffer.
2. Neither of you should wear your wedding ring before the ceremony.
3. You shouldn't buy the engagement and wedding rings at the same time.
4. Don't show the wedding dress to anyone but your mother.
5. It's bad luck for the groom to see you in your wedding dress before the ceremony.

ETHNIC CUSTOMS FROM AROUND THE WORLD

You can personalize your own festivities by incorporating some of the traditions from your ethnic backgrounds, or from any that appeal to you.

In colonial *America* it was believed that whoever made the first purchase after the ceremony would 'rule the nest'. Brides would buy a pin from a bridesmaid as soon as they reached the church door. Another popular conviction was that the weather throughout the bride's day would reflect the pattern of her future life. A beautiful morning but stormy afternoon meant a good beginning but trouble later. In the nineteenth-century South it was believed that whoever first rose from the altar would be the first to die. At many receptions today the guests will bang on their dishes or glasses until the bride and groom kiss.

Chinese grooms felt that they would rule the future relationship if they were able to sit on part of their new wife's dress when they seated themselves on the bridal bed. Red, the Chinese color of good luck is still used throughout the wedding celebration, from gowns to invitations.

Egyptian wedding guests toss flowers at the couple as they enter the reception hall. Each flower is believed to bring a moment of good luck to the marriage.

During the days of the first Queen Elizabeth, the *English* would make a stack of little cakes. The bride and groom had to reach over the pile and kiss. The object was to keep the stack from falling for as long as possible. When it eventually did the guests pelted them with the cakes, then ate the pieces.

Brides of *Finland* would wear a crown. At the end of the wedding festivities the unmarried girls would blindfold her, form a circle and dance around the bride, singing along with all the guests, "It has been, it has gone, never will the bride be a maid more, never will she dance with the crown again." The bride then reaches out and crowns a girl. It was believed she would be the next to wed.

German grooms would show their dominance by kneeling on the bride's dress hem at the altar. She could counter his action by standing on his foot when they rose again. When they returned from the church a beer stein would be hurled over the roof to keep the groom from drinking too much. He would carry his bride over the threshold, and inside they shared a morsel of bread to ensure they would always have enough to eat. The groom then pushed the bride into the kitchen, where she began her wifely role by salting a pot of soup. At the reception, the toastmaster called the name of each guest. They came forward, gave their gift, then took a drink from a jug. When this was finished, the bride rose, made an exclamation of pain, and took off her shoe. To her surprise, there was a coin there. She presented it to the musicians, who then began to play. After the bride danced with the groom and both fathers, three candles are lit and placed on the floor. She dances with each of her husband's relatives in turn. If the candles stayed lit throughout these dances, the couple will have a happy future.

Many *Greek* brides still put up a struggle as they are carried over the threshold. This tradition is left over from the days when brides were captured. They would also carry a lump of sugar in their glove to ensure sweetness all their married lives. The Handkerchief Dance is still popular today. A crowd of guests is led by a dancer singing and waving a handkerchief. As they follow him he occasionally moves out of the chain to make intricate leaps and jumps.

In *India,* a coconut was passed three times over the bride and groom, then shattered on the ground to drive away demons.

In ancient *Israel* the bride wore a blue ribbon to signify her fidelity. That is the origin of our current custom of wearing 'something blue'. Another custom was for her shoes to be exchanged between the groom and the bride's father as a symbol of the transfer to a new home. It's believed this was the origin of tying old shoes on the back of the get-away car. Today the folk dance "Hora" is popular at all Jewish weddings. Guests gather around the couple and skip and kick to the music as they move in a circle. The most popular song for the Hora is "Hava Nagila". At one point the bride and groom usually start to lead the line of dancers in a weaving parade around the room.

Long ago in *Italy,* the guests would toss sugared almonds at the couple in hopes to bring them sweetness and prosperity. Many Italian brides incorporate that custom in their weddings today by placing a few sugared almonds at each place setting. Ideally, everyone at the wedding will eat them at the same time as a token of the happiness you all share that day.

Japanese couples take nine sips of sake as part of their ceremony. They are married after the first sip. The sake is poured into three different cups from a double-spouted kettle decorated with butterflies to signify that they will share everything.

During the *Mexican* wedding ceremony, the groom would present the bride with thirteen gold coins to symbolize his ability to support her. A chain of flowers, called the 'Laso' is looped at each end. One end is slipped over the bride's head, the other over the groom's to symbolize their unity.

At *Polish* weddings, the bride and groom lead their guests in a "Grand March" by parading around the room to the beat of music. After several passes, they stop at the end of a long table filled with pieces of cake, cigars, and shots of whiskey. The guests line up to greet the bride and groom, and many grab a shot for themselves and one for the new couple to salute them with a drink. Another popular custom is for the guests to gather in a large circle holding hands and singing "Let Me Call You Sweetheart" while the bride and groom dance their last dance together before they leave the festivities.

In *Switzerland,* and many other European countries noisy parties were held on the eve of the wedding. The evening was filled with music, eating, and dancing, and no one slept lest the evil spirits strike. The party usually ended with lots of noise to drive the spirits away—often all the crockery and the windows of the house were broken.

Welsh bridesmaids would plant a sprig from the bride's bouquet on either side of the couple's front door. If the sprig took, there'd be another wedding when the bush bloomed. If it didn't, the planter would be an old maid.

Finishing Touches

Your Wedding Party

Asking friends and family to help you on your wedding day isn't only an ancient custom, it's a way to receive encouragement and support, and to share in the fun-filled atmosphere of the day.

You only need two witnesses to the ceremony. The male witness is called the best man, the female witness is the maid of honor. The number of attendants depends on the style of your wedding and personal preference. A large, formal wedding would require a much larger wedding party than a small, informal one because ushers are needed to seat the guests. See **Wedding Styles** section for the average number of attendants at each type of wedding.

Family members usually receive priority over friends, but most couples try to mix the two. It's also considered thoughtful if you each ask a few members of the other's family to join your wedding party (bride's brother as groomsman, groom's sister as bridesmaid) even if you don't know them well. You never have to feel obligated to invite a person merely because you were in their wedding party. No rule of etiquette requires it, nor should it be expected of you. It's not necessary to have the same number of ushers as bridesmaids, although it shouldn't be overly imbalanced (such as eight bridesmaids and two ushers).

The obligations of the members of the wedding party are listed below. Remember, not everyone is aware of these responsibilities—especially if they've never been in a wedding before. Don't assume. Don't hesitate to talk about the duties and responsibilities when you ask someone to stand up. It could save confusion and hurt feelings later. In addition, you can change and adjust their roles to suit your personal needs. Do you need them to hold your hand at an out of town shower? Keep you company the night before the wedding? Let them know your expectations.

All attendants are expected to pay for their own attire, transportation to your town, and a gift for you. You provide their flowers, and any extras such as parasols. If they are from out of town, you should arrange and pay for their lodging. The bridesmaids and honor attendant usually assemble at your home about one hour before you leave for the ceremony. You are responsible for their transportation for the rest of the day.

Remember that although they care about you, your attendants are not going to be as obsessed with your wedding as you are, nor should they go bankrupt trying to keep up with your plans. They should assist you, but they're not your slaves. These are supposed to be people you care about. Don't expect more than is reasonable from any of them. If you know that this wedding is a huge drain on their budget, be considerate and tell them their presence is present enough.

MAID OR MATRON OF HONOR

Some brides have two honor attendants and divide their duties. An unmarried woman is a maid, a married woman is a matron. She will help the bride in every way needed during preparations. In addition, she usually hosts one or two showers for the bride and attends all others possible. Hers is one of the most important roles in the wedding. She stays near you throughout your wedding day, and her job is to provide support, keep you calm, and make sure that you and your clothes are picture perfect at all times. During the ceremony she will hold your bouquet and the groom's ring. If you wear a blusher veil she lifts it back at the appropriate time. She is usually dressed in a slightly different manner than the other female attendants—whether in a gown of a distinctive style, color, or pattern.

You can choose any female for this role whether it's your sister, best friend, or cousin. Some brides choose their mothers, but many feel that's improper if you're having a large reception since she's the official hostess. If you do have two honor attendants, be sure to indicate to each what their duties will be. Years ago an honor attendant was not supposed to be a widow or divorcee, but that custom has long disappeared. Her traditional duties include:

- ☐ Assists in making the arrangements if you ask for help.
- ☐ Works to make it a problem-free occasion.
- ☐ Reminds you about details, such as ordering invitations and arranging for the announcements.
- ☐ Attends (and hosts) pre-wedding festivities.
- ☐ Makes sure your attire and appearance are perfect throughout the day.
- ☐ Arranges and pays for her own clothing.
- ☐ Hosts a personal shower for you.
- ☐ Stays near you and provides assistance whenever necessary on your wedding day.
- ☐ Helps you to dress the morning of the wedding and gets you to the church punctually.
- ☐ Stands near you during the ceremony, holds your bouquet.
- ☐ Holds the groom's ring at the ceremony, and witnesses the marriage license.
- ☐ Makes sure your hat, coat, gloves, or other personal items aren't left at the church.
- ☐ Stands in the receiving line.
- ☐ Helps you bustle your gown for the reception.
- ☐ Dances with the groom (after the bride, groom's mother, and bride's mother have had their turn), then with both fathers, best man, and other male attendants.
- ☐ Offers help to family and guests whenever needed. Draws lonely guests into the festivities.
- ☐ Helps you change into your going away clothes.
- ☐ Assists you and the groom in leaving the reception smoothly.
- ☐ In some traditions she might lift your blusher veil at the altar, and ceremoniously remove your veil at the reception.

BRIDESMAIDS

Bridesmaids assist you in the preparations, and should phone periodically to see if there are any errands they can run. They could also help by addressing envelopes for the invitations and announcements. Most of their duties are concerned with showers and parties before the wedding. They may host a few showers, and are expected to attend as many activities as possible. They're also the bride's support group on her wedding day. They add to the festivity and join in the fun from decorating to dancing. They should be charming to guests, and circulate among them during the reception. Many couples pair a bridesmaid with a groomsman to escort her throughout the day. A junior bridesmaid is a girl from ten to fourteen years of age. She can dress the same as the other bridesmaids, or slightly different. It's entirely optional whether you would assign a groomsman to escort her.

FLOWER GIRL

Traditionally a young girl (between four and ten) preceded the bride up the aisle scattering rose petals. Most ceremony sites forbid this practice, but the flower girl still adds a lovely balance to the wedding—and it is almost always a huge thrill for the girl. She wears a short pretty dress that matches the general style of the wedding attire. She can wear a floral headband, wreath, haircomb, or hat to compliment her outfit. Most girls carry a basket of flowers.

BEST MAN

He's the essential male attendant, responsible for handling arrangements, bolstering his confidence, and supplying reassurance. He can be a brother, cousin, friend, uncle—even the groom's father. It's most important that he be reliable. His traditional duties are:

☐ Assists him with necessary arrangements. Does whatever he can to make it a smooth, problem-free occasion.
☐ Attends pre-wedding festivities.
☐ Makes sure groom's formalwear attire is selected and picked up before the wedding, returned after the wedding.
☐ Reminds him about details, such as ordering flowers and obtaining the marriage license.
☐ Arranges and pays for his personal formal attire.
☐ Hosts the bachelor party.
☐ Stays near the groom and provides assistance whenever necessary on the wedding day.
☐ Helps him to dress the morning of the wedding and gets him to the church punctually.
☐ Stands near him during the ceremony.
☐ Holds your ring and the marriage license at the ceremony, and witnesses the license.
☐ Distributes fees for clergyman, cantor, church, organist, and tips for others (such as altar servers) after the ceremony.
☐ Escorts the maid of honor in the processional and recessional (if that conforms to your wedding style).
☐ Makes sure the groom's hat, coat, gloves, or other personal items aren't left at the church.
☐ Stands in the receiving line.
☐ As master of ceremonies of the reception dinner, he introduces the wedding party, minister, speakers, and reads any congratulatory telegrams.
☐ Proposes the first toast to the new couple. Acts as toastmaster and keeps things moving if a number of toasts are offered.
☐ Dances with the bride (after the groom, his father, and bride's father have had their turn). Then with both mothers, maid of honor, and other female attendants.
☐ Offers help to family and guests whenever needed.
☐ Protects the luggage and getaway car from pranksters, has it ready for when you leave.
☐ Helps you exit the reception smoothly.
☐ Holds onto your honeymoon tickets if you're leaving right away, and verifies you have them before you leave.

USHERS/ GROOMSMEN

This role is a combined one at many weddings today. But by definition, an usher seats the guests at the wedding ceremony, a groomsman escorts a bridesmaid in the processional/recessional. You need one usher to seat every fifty guests. You can assume one-half to three-fourths of your invited guests will attend the ceremony. Here are their duties:

☐ Be fitted, pick up, and pay for their formal attire.
☐ Attends pre-wedding parties of mixed company, including the bachelor party and rehearsal dinner.
☐ Attends rehearsal.
☐ Transports bridesmaids and out of town guests throughout the wedding day.
☐ Lends a hand whenever needed.
☐ Stays available for formal pictures at the ceremony and reception.
☐ Arrives at ceremony site approximately one hour before it's to begin.
☐ Seats the guests. (See Ceremony Seating section).
☐ Passes out ceremony programs (if any) to the guests.
☐ Unrolls aisle carpet.
☐ Either precedes or escorts the bridesmaids up the aisle in the processional and recessional.
☐ Bows out the rows of guests after the recessional.
☐ After the ceremony is over and the guests have left, the ushers removes pew markers, programs, and checks the seats for personal items left behind.
☐ In many areas it's traditional for the bridesmaids, groomsmen, and ushers to festively decorate the couple's car after the ceremony.
☐ Be attentive and helpful to other members of the wedding party and guests throughout the day.

You may want to photocopy the information about ceremony seating that can be found in the **Ceremony Details** chapter and have your fiance distribute it to the ushers.

RINGBEARER/PAGE

These roles are filled by young boys who are usually between the ages of four and ten. The ring bearer carries a satin pillow with the wedding rings tied or sewn on. Pages are rare today; their main purpose was to carry the bride's extremely long train. However, most bride's have shorter trains so they are seldom necessary.

BRIDE'S PARENTS

They are the official hosts of the wedding day. Your mother helps with the planning, is responsible for the guest list for your side of the family, and is usually a clearing house for questions about the wedding. Once she's chosen the style and color of her dress, she informs the groom's mother so she can choose hers. It's also a nice idea for her to maintain some kind of contact with the groom's mother, and keep her up to date with the planning details.

She's the last person seated before the wedding processional begins, and stands at the head of the receiving line at the reception.

Your father often rides with you to the ceremony, and traditionally escorts you in the processional. He can stand in the receiving line, but it isn't required. In some regions, it's customary for him to provide cigars and whiskey shots to toast the couple after the Grand March of the reception.

GROOM'S PARENTS

They contact the bride's family after the engagement is announced, and welcome her into the family. It's a nice idea to arrange a visit, or exchange letters and phone calls between the families. Wedding days run much more smoothly when the families are acquainted. Traditionally, they host a dinner for the wedding party and guests after the rehearsal.

Your mother gets first choice on clothing style, and ideally the groom's mother will co-ordinate hers by wearing the same length, basic style, and a complimentary color. His father usually dresses in the same manner as the other men in the wedding party—although he doesn't have to match exactly.

The groom's mom is responsible for producing the guest list for their side of the family, after she's been told the number of slots available.

They're co-hosts of the reception, whether they contributed financially or not. His mother stands in the receiving line to welcome and introduce guests from his side of the family (his father can also stand in the line if he wants to).

Both sets of parents should circulate, be available for photographs, and traditional events such as the cake cutting.

WAYS TO HONOR OTHER FRIENDS OR FAMILY MEMBERS

- Ask their help with decisions, decorations.
- Have them read from scripture, or a poem, at the ceremony.
- Serve as candle lighters at ceremony.
- Be in charge of guest book at reception.
- Offer special toast to them at reception.

Finding the Perfect Dress

How many times have you imagined yourself in your wedding gown? Dreamed about wearing one that you saw in a bridal magazine? Those fantasies will help form an important basis for selecting the perfect wedding dress. There is probably a certain type of gown that you see yourself wearing. Do you want to look like a Victorian maiden? A country girl? A princess? A queen? A sophisticated lady? Or are you having trouble making up your mind?

When you shop, you're not just buying a dress—but a whole ensemble: gown, headpiece, undergarments, and shoes. They will probably cost more than any outfit you have owned in the past or will purchase in the future. Most importantly, the style of your apparel will set the pattern for guests and members of the wedding party. Obviously, you should take your time in making this important purchase!

VOCABULARY GUIDE

If you are not well-versed in fashion terms or descriptions of the different materials, I've included a list of the more common terms for your convenience.

A-Line Skirt	Close fitting waist slowly tapers to a flared hem.
Alencon Lace	Needlepoint lace of solid design on a net background. Usually in floral or paisley patterns.
Antebellum Waist	Dress has natural waistline that dips two inches to a point in the center front.
Asymmetrical	Fabric falls to one side from the natural waistline.
Ballerina Skirt	Full skirt that reveals the ankles.
Ballet Length	Falls just above the ankles.
Basque Waistline	Waistline of dress is two inches below the natural waist, and often dips to a point in the center front.
Bateau Neckline	A straight line across the collarbone to just before the tip of the shoulders.
Batiste	Soft, delicate summer fabric made of cotton or cotton-linen blend. Texture is fine and sheer.
Bell Sleeve	Long sleeve that flares gently from the shoulder to the wrist.
Bell Skirt	A circular cut, usually in a longer length.
Bertha Collar	Cape of fabric or lace attached to neckline for a shawl effect.

Bishop Sleeve	Full sleeve that ends in a gathered band at the wrist.
Blouson	Drooping fullness in fabric from the bodice to the waist, gathered at or below the waist.
Blusher Veil	The short veil that covers the bride's face during the processional.
Bouffant	A full, flaring skirt.
Brocade	Winter dress fabric of silk, cotton, wool, or linen with woven patterns of raised yarn. Price can vary depending on the quality and weight of the material.
Brush Train	Very short train that just sweeps the floor as you walk.
Brussels Lace	Light, delicate, with subtle patterns, this is very beautiful and extremely expensive trimming.
Bustle Back	Exaggerated fullness in the rear of the skirt, built with a pad or frame. Often done with the bridal train for easier movement at the reception.
Cap Sleeve	Short, barely covers the top of the arm.
Capelet Sleeve	Falls several inches below the elbow in a soft flare.
Caplet Train	Flows from the back of the shoulders.
Cathedral Train	Material extends three yards from the waist.
Chantilly Lace	Soft, fragile, usually in web-like patterns, this lace is very costly.
Chapel Train	Extends up to four feet from the waist.
Cluny Lace	Made of fine linen thread, usually in open designs.
Court Train	Extends a little under three feet from the waist.
Crepe	Soft, fluid, summer fabric of silk, cotton, polyester, or rayon. The texture is finely crinkled or ridged.
Crepe De Chine	Soft, light, thin fabric of silk, rayon, or polyester. Used for informal gowns in fall or winter, it's the same material used to make many blouses.
Crinoline	Underskirt foundation used to extend skirt.
Detachable Train	Joined to the gown at the waistline with hooks and eyes, can be removed for the reception.
Dolman Sleeve	Top of the sleeve is wide, cut in one piece with the shoulder.
Drop Waist	Waistline of dress is several inches below the natural waist.
Embroidered Organza	Patterns of flowers with rolled edges that are often lightly color tinted.
Empire Waist	High-waisted dress with a short bodice. The skirt begins two or more inches above the natural waistline.
English Net	Fine, sheer cotton netting, traditional but expensive fabric for wedding gowns.
Eyelet	Silk, cotton, or cotton-polyester fabric used in Spring and Summer weddings. It is decorated by small, round, holes finished at the edges with lace and/or embroidery.
Faille	A heavier fabric for fall or winter weddings it is rather stiff in texture, with a slightly rib-like weave. Made of silk, rayon, or polyester blend.
Fitted Sleeve	Narrow, long sleeve.
Floor Length	Hemline falls 1/2 to 1 1/2 inches from the floor.
Full Skirt	Gathered, but less full than bouffant style.
Gauntlet	Covers arm and wrist with lace or fabric. Used in place of gloves (they're fingerless).
Georgette	Silk or synthetic crepe with a dull texture.
Gibson Sleeve	Full at the shoulder, fitted at the wrist.

Hoopskirt	Underskirt is stiffened with circular hoops.
Illusion	A silk tulle fabric used primarily for veils.
Jersey	Soft, fluid material made of wool, silk, or rayon. Usually has a satin or matte finish.
Jewel Neckline	Fabric circles the natural neckline.
Juliet Cap	Headpiece fits snugly over the crown.
Leg Of Mutton Sleeve	Very full puff at the shoulder, becomes tightly fitted on the forearm.
Net	Open thread-weave fabric often used in veils.
Organdy	Cotton muslin summer fabric of a thin, fine weave. Has a stiff texture and crisp finish.
Organza	Plain weave style fabric made of silk or synthetic fibers.
Peau De Soie	Winter dress material made of blended fabrics. Has a light, silky texture and a dull, satin-like finish.
Peek-a-boo Sleeve	Sheer puffed sleeve that has a different fabric showing through underneath.
Peplum	Short flounce or overskirt attached at the waistline.
Poet Sleeve	Style is pleated at the shoulder, very full from shoulder to cuff.
Point D'esprit	Net or tulle with dots woven into the pattern.
Pointed Sleeve	Long, fitted sleeve that falls into a point below the wrist and over the top of the hand.
Poly-Organza	Good summer weight fabric, doesn't wrinkle easily. Look for double-layer construction.
Poly-Silk Chiffon	Used in dress styles with multi-layered skirts, this summer fabric is sheer, with a tissue-like texture. More durable than silk chiffon, the material still stretches enough to make it impossible to hang on a hanger.
Poly-Silk Organza	Blended summer fabric that is sheer, crisp, and less likely to wrinkle than silk organza.
Princess Line	Dress style with slightly flared design that accentuates the waist, but doesn't hug the body.
Puff Sleeve	Short, full sleeve that ends above the elbow, usually gathered at the bottom.
Queen Anne Neckline	Design is high on the sides and back, with an open bodice in a sweetheart shape.
Queen Elizabeth	High collar stands up in back, comes to a closed v in front.
Raised Waist	Waistline about one inch above the natural waistline.
Rayon Satin	Blended fabric with a shiny finish used for winter gowns. It has a tendency to unravel at the seams if it's not properly reinforced.
Royal Train	The longest, more than three yards of material extend from the waist.
Sabrina Neckline	Begins two inches inside the shoulder, and is straight across the front.
Satin	Silk or synthetic material with a smooth, usually shiny, unbroken surface.
Schiffli Embroidery	Expensive machine made lace, usually in fine, delicate patterns. The best is made from a cotton-polyester fiber base.
Scoop Neckline	Round, low, neckline.
Sheath	A silhouette of straight, slim, lines.
Shirred Waist	Fabric is gathered to make a horizontal panel at the waist.

Silk Chiffon	Sheer tissue-like fabric usually used in dresses styled with multi-layered skirts. Used for Spring and Summer weddings, this is a material that easily stretches out of shape. Don't hang it on a hanger.
Silk Faced Satin	Traditional material for many winter weddings, this is a heavy fabric with a rich sheen.
Silk Organza	Sheer, crisp material used for gowns worn in Spring or Summer. It wrinkles very easily.
Sweep Train	Slightly longer than a brush train.
Sweetheart Neckline	Begins two inches inside the shoulder line, and dips to heart shape in the center of the bodice.
Taffeta	Lustrous material of crisp, plain or finely ribbed weave. Usually made of silk, rayon, or a silk-polyester blend.
Tea Length	Gown falls several inches above the ankles.
Tiered Skirt	Skirt has a series of layered panels falling in graduated lengths.
Train	Fabric from the gown that trails behind the bride as she walks.
Trumpet Skirt	Tapers close to the legs, then flared at or below the knee (think of a mermaid).
Tulle	Thin, floaty, fabric of fine, small-meshed net. Made of silk, rayon, or nylon. Used in dresses that have a many-layered full skirt.
Velvet	A cold weather fabric made of silk, cotton, or a silk-cotton blend. In lower quality fabrics, nylon is used as part of the blend. The fiber is a thick, soft pile with a matte finish.
Venise Lace	Cotton or linen lace with a heavy texture, usually made in leaf, or floral patterns.
Victorian	Typical gowns worn in the latter half of the nineteenth century.
Voile	Light, open-weave fabric of wool, silk, cotton, or cotton polyester blend. Used for informal dress styles.
Watteau	Train falls from the back yoke of the dress.
Wedding Band Collar	Upright collar encircles the base of the neck, often made of lace.

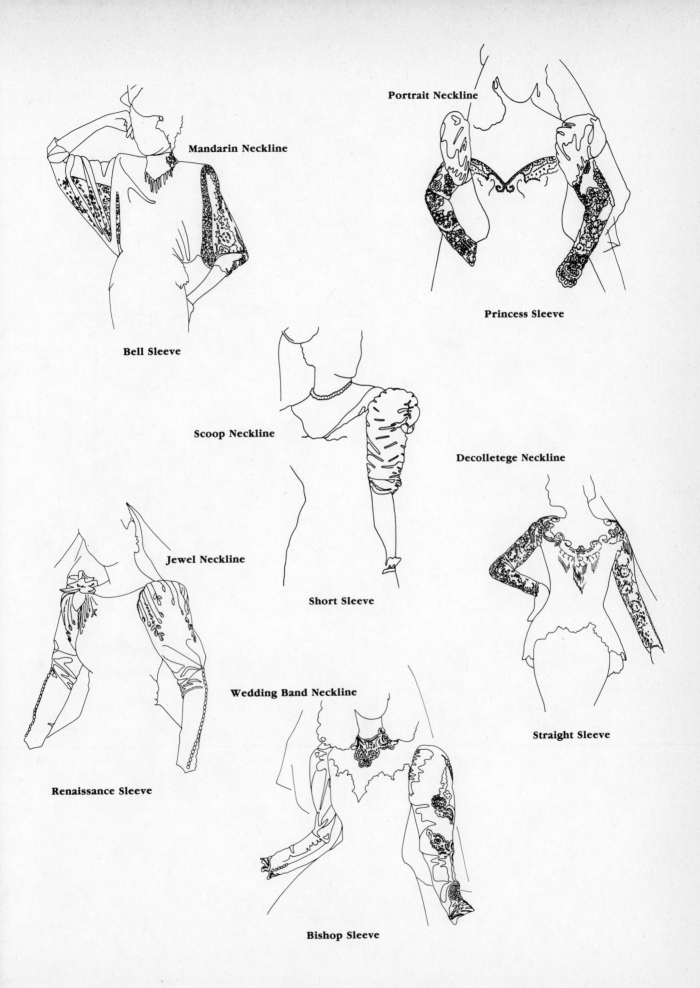

Mandarin Neckline

Portrait Neckline

Princess Sleeve

Bell Sleeve

Scoop Neckline

Decolletege Neckline

Jewel Neckline

Short Sleeve

Straight Sleeve

Renaissance Sleeve

Wedding Band Neckline

Bishop Sleeve

67

A-Line

Narrow

Demi-Belle

Bouffant

Shirtwaist

Princess

69

WHERE TO LOOK

Bridal salons and more exclusive department stores feature custom made gowns. You try on a sample, and when you find the one you want they take your measurements. The dress is made to suit your figure. Although you can make changes to your gown (the style of sleeve, length of train, etc.) it's generally less expensive to keep looking. You may find the perfect dress that doesn't need expensive alterations!

You can also purchase off-the-rack apparel through department stores or catalogs. They are usually made in bulk in a variety of sizes. Since decorations are sewn by machine, they don't have the detailed handiwork found in custom made gowns. Only minor alterations can be done, such as shortening the hem or adding a dart to the bodice.

Another alternative is to purchase a pattern and material and sew your own —or have it sewn. Make sure that the design and trim are commiserate with the skills of the seamstress. If you hire someone to sew the gown, have a back-up available in case a problem occurs before she completes the dress.

For more limited budgets you may purchase a second-hand dress from a resale shop or newspaper advertisement; or borrow the one that your mother, aunt, sister, or grandmother wore.

Allow several days to visit shops and try on dresses. Don't try to look at too many in one day, you'll only get tired and confused. You don't want to end up choosing prematurely just to get it over with. If you'll be visiting a bridal salon or exclusive department store, make an appointment to be sure you'll receive adequate attention. Tell them your budget, and ask that they only show items in your price range. Choosing a gown is an emotional experience and it's easy to get swept away when you're wearing an extravagant style made of expensive material. To share your excitement and add balance and perspective to your choices, have your mother and maid of honor accompany you. They can help by offering advice, suggestions, and opinions on whether the dress suits you. Of course, you make the final decision.

At the shop, you and your companions will be placed in a large dressing room. Gowns will be brought to you for inspection, and you select the ones you wish to try on. Don't reject them too quickly, some dresses will look much more attractive on you than on the hanger. In addition, you may think you want a certain style of gown, then discover that a completely different design looks best once you've tried it on. You can sample as many as you like, and there are always other stores.

You may be told that "you'll know" when you try on the perfect dress. Perhaps—but few brides are that sure of themselves immediately. It's especially hard to trust your judgement if you've already tried on a large number of gowns. Don't be surprised if you go back to the shop a week after you selected that perfect gown—because you forgot what it looked like!

WHAT STYLE IS RIGHT FOR YOU?

Every dress has details that make it special—whether it's the layered skirt, embroidered sleeve, or ruffled hem. As you search among the available designs it will be a combination of these elements that will catch your eye. Most importantly, your dress should make you look attractive and suit your personality. Study the effect of each gown. Is it flattering to your figure? How does it move? What does the back look like? (Remember your guests will be staring at it during the ceremony). Here is some additional information of how best to accentuate your shape and size (consult the Vocabulary Guide for any definitions needed):

Short The following will create an illusion of height: Empire waistline; appliques running up and down the length of the dress; a high neckline, or trim at the neck and shoulders; short sleeves or sleeveless with long gloves; a chapel train with floor length veil. Frills and excessive detailing are not for you.

Tall To minimize your height: Wear a skirt with many tiers or flounces; low neck; raglan sleeve; close fitting cap; or brimmed hat.

Thin Fill out your figure with a full princess style, or one with a basque waist and full skirt. Add the illusion of pounds with full, long sleeves, bloused bodice, and gathered skirt. Softly draping materials such as jersey, satin, or velvet will also help.

Top Heavy Balance your figure by drawing the eye down and lengthening the upper body. Elongated bodices with basque waistlines are ideal; and a full, billowing skirt with lots of ornamentation will create a curvier lower body. Keep sleeves simple with a natural shoulder line, and avoid adornments on the bodice. Stay away from low necklines, heavily decorated bodices, big, full sleeves, and empire style dresses.

Pear Shape Narrow above the waist and heavy below, you want a gown with a long, textured bodice with lots of trim. This will create the illusion of a fuller upper body, and draw the eyes to that area. Full sleeves that extend the shoulder line will also help. The skirt should accentuate the waist, then be unadorned with a controlled fullness. Stay away from slim, sheath silhouettes, very full skirts, lots of ornamentation in the hip area, and high necklines (they make the shoulders look narrower and will throw you off balance).

Stick Figure You need to create a shape if you have no waist, with bust and hips equally sized. Ornamentation should appear on both upper and lower body to provide balance in both areas. Gowns with oversized shoulders, a jewel or bateau neckline, and elaborately detailed sleeves are best. You want voluminous skirt with horizontal styling. Try and obtain a fabric that will hold its shape, such as taffeta. Avoid high-waisted dresses, or slim silhouettes with vertical styling. They'll make you appear taller and thinner.

Full Figure Avoid clingy fabrics such as those just recommended for thin figures. A floating material such as chiffon will camouflage the extra pounds. Don't select a gown with full bouffant skirt and flounces, or with contrasting colors, such as a white gown with a pink waistline. It's best to try a princess style that just skims the body, or an empire with an a-line skirt. Look for a v or shallow u neckline, slender (but not tight) sleeves, an a-line skirt silhouette, and a detached train. To minimize a thick midriff or waist, use a lifted waistline and a-line skirt. Broad shoulders can be toned down with a bare neckline, or one draped with a wide collar. If you want to minimize a large bosom, avoid styles that gather directly under the bust. A high neck, such as a Victorian neckline will also pull the eye away from the bustline. Avoid a lot of lace and beading—it will make the dress, (and you) look heavier.

Hourglass Your bust and hip measurements are equal, and your waist is about ten inches smaller than either of those measurements. Make the most of that waist by balancing proportions in simple, classic lines. Off the shoulder sleeves and plunging necklines are fine. You don't want too much ornamentation on the bodice or skirt—they can make you look too heavy. An empire style would hide all your good points.

COLOR

Make sure that the gown's color is flattering on you. Most dresses are off-white, bright white, or ivory. However, an ivory gown can make some complexion tones look washed out, or make others look yellow.

DETERMINING A PROPER FIT

Neck
No style should be so loose that it puckers at the neck. A rounded neckline should settle at the hollow base of your throat.

Bust
Bodice should lay smoothly across your bosom. If it is a fitted style, it should be snug—but not too tight. Darts should be in line with the fullest part of your bosom. Side seams should hang from armhole to hem in a straight line.

Sleeve
If your sleeve style is supposed to fit tightly there's no way around the fact that arm movements will be difficult. All other sleeve styles should feel comfortable. The cuff rests at your wristbone, with any lace or trim extending over your upper hand. Shoulder seams should lie on top of the shoulders and be invisible at the front of the dress.

Waist
If there are bubbles or wrinkles, the dress is too long-waisted and should be altered.

Length
Gown should be 1 1/2 to 2 inches off the floor when you are wearing your shoes. The entire dress should hang gracefully and move with you when you are in motion.

Make sure that the measurements are taken accurately. You'll have to make a general decision about alterations and the need for extra length. Don't get carried away and order a much smaller size—thinking you'll lose the weight before the wedding. This is going to be a nervous, hectic time for you, and the reality is that you probably won't. Not only is it a lot easier to take a dress in than to let it out—the whole point of a custom made dress is that it will have a beautiful fit.

You will return for one or two fittings after the dress comes in. Make sure that you bring shoes the same height as those you'll wear at your wedding, so the proper hem length can be determined. You'll also want to be fitted in the undergarments you'll wear on your wedding day. Does the gown fit comfortably? Zipper work properly? Are all the buttons and hooks in their proper places? If you will have your dress bustled for the reception, ask the seamstress to show you how it must be done. (If possible bring your maid of honor along for the final fitting, since she'll probably be the one to bustle your dress).

COST

Price will be based on the intricacy of the dress's style, the type of material, the amount of trimwork and it's value, and the number of alterations made to the original design. Custom made gowns are the most expensive, least expensive are those you make yourself, purchase second-hand, or borrow.

English net, silk organza, silk chiffon, or silk-faced satin are the most expensive fabrics. In the middle range are poly-organza, poly-silk organza, faille, peu de soie, taffeta, and tulle. Least expense are gowns of batiste, jersey, rayon, satin, eyelet, organdy, crepe, velvet, poly-silk chiffon, and voile.

Many dresses are made of a combination of materials to keep costs down. While a taffeta gown is quite expensive, a dress with a polyester-chiffon overskirt and taffeta underskirt can be quite reasonably priced.

Different trimmings can drive the cost of the dress sky high. If you add the fine detail of imported Brussels or Chantilly lace to your gown—you can break the bank. Machine made polyester lace, on the other hand, is quite inexpensive.

Examine your dress carefully. How nicely are the buttons, zippers, and seams put together? Are laces glued on? Beads pasted? The cost of the gown should be much less if they are.

ORDERING

If you are having the dress made, try to have it started at least six months before the wedding. You need to allow for possible delays (mechanical or labor difficulties, heavy orders for June through August). Most brides have a formal portrait done a month before the wedding, naturally you want to be sure it's completed by that date. You must also allow time for fittings, any final alterations, and pressing. It's certainly possible to obtain a gown in less time, but you will limit your choices and open yourself up for potential problems and expense.

Be sure to total all items—dress, alterations, headpiece and veil, before you make your decision. These can add up quickly and may break your budget before you realize it.

You'll be asked to place a deposit on the ensemble you select, and most shops will not order the gown until you have paid at least half of the price. Discuss payment arrangements. Must you pay every two weeks? What happens if you don't? Find out the estimated date for your dress to arrive, and charges for alterations and pressing. Don't be afraid to ask what happens if you cancel the order before the dress arrives. (You might find the perfect dress elsewhere, break the engagement, or elope).

Some stores allow a five day cancellation period, others order immediately and you will forfeit your deposit if you cancel. Obtain a receipt where the delivery date of the dress and headpiece is clearly indicated—and read every word before you sign anything!

YOUR HEADPIECE

Your bridal ensemble won't be complete until you select your headpiece and veil. Be sure to try it on while you're wearing the dress. The style, color, and trim ornamentation of lace, embroidery, and beads, should match your gown. For example: If your gown is decorated with seed pearls, some should appear on your headpiece. For best results, style your hair as closely as possible to the way you plan to wear it on your wedding day. Just as with dresses, many headpiece styles will look better on you than in the clerk's hands, so try on lots of different designs. Your final selection should also complement your facial features and suit your hairstyle.

Almost every headpiece has two principle parts. A cap piece or hat, and veiling. The cap might be covered with fabric, flowers, lace, jewels, seed pearls, rhinestones, sequins, or crystal beads. Russian veiling, (often used with hats) has a widely spaced weave with diamond-shaped holes usually made of a heavier thread. Illusion veiling is the fabric for the standard long veil that the traditional bride wears. It's made of a tighter weave in nylon or silk tulle. The best quality have the highest content of silk in the fabric, and the tiniest holes.

What will look best? The only way to know is to try it on. Generally, the wide brim and low crown of a garden hat will abbreviate a long face. If your face is round, you can lengthen it with a high tiara or pillbox hat. If you have a short, full figure, stay away from billowy veils—they will only accentuate your size.

Practice turning and bending while wearing your headpiece and veil. You can have a comb, or extra combs sewn in if you are having trouble making it stay on properly.
The following illustrations offer some of the types of hats available.

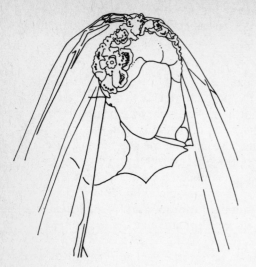

Face Framing

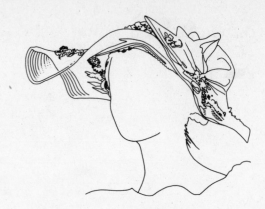

Garden Hat

Tudor Hat

Tiara

Headband Cap

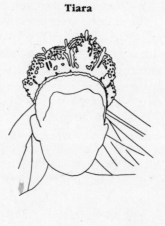

Haircomb

Bow

74

Here are descriptions of each:

Banana Clip is a curved hair ornament with a spring grip to hold a large section of hair. Embellished with silk flowers, beading, jewels, or tulle veiling.

A *Bow* of looped ribbon or elegant fabric might be worn at the nape of the neck, or on the crown. Usually decorated with ribbon, streamers, or bead ornamentation.

Crown pieces are a traditional half-circle set toward the front of the head. They look very attractive with princess or bouffant style gowns. Although they can be worn with any type of hairdo, these look best with very short and straight hair.

Derby Hats have a rounded crown and narrow brim. They are worn straight across the head, look best with ruffly, old-fashioned gowns. Hair should be worn pinned up, or slightly off the face.

The *Forehead band* has a strip of decorated fabric (usually beaded) that is worn across the forehead. Looks best with shorter hairstyles and sophisticated gown styles.

Garden Hats have a larger, round crown and a wide brim. They look prettiest with long, full, curly hair and should be worn straight across the head and low over the brow. Wear it with a Victorian or Country-Style dress that has lots of ruffles and flounces. (Remember that a large-brimmed hat will cast shadows over your face in the photographs. You'll want to pin back the brim for pictures).

Half Hats are slightly larger than the Juliet Caps, and fit tightly on the head at mid crown. Look great with short, curly hair and any dress style.

A *Haircomb* decorated with a cluster of silk flowers and other trimmings might be worn at the side or back of the head. It looks very nice with hair pulled back, can be worn with a number of different gowns.

Headband Caps frame the face with a wide strip covered with ornamentation. They're worn on top of the head in front of the ears. The style goes very well with any type of dress, and looks best with hairstyles that have bangs.

Juliet Caps are small and snug-fitting. They sit at the back of the head and look lovely with short, curly hair. They blend nicely with formal, traditional gowns.

Mantilla Veils sometimes have a small cap underneath to add height. A decorated border (usually of intricate lace) frames the face and brow. Wear with any traditional style gown that has a simple bodice and neckline. Looks best with hair either long and flowing or pinned up.

Pillbox Hats are small and brimless with a round, flat crown. Worn straight across the head, they look nicest with short hair, or a chignon. They suit modern, sophisticated styles, tailored looks.

Snoods are delicate netting which cover your hair. A more contemporary alternative to veils, they're often fronted by a headband, and decorated with bows, pearls, and flowers. They look best with shoulder length hair.

Tudor Hats have a somewhat peaked crown with a narrow brim at the front. Wear it straight across the head over the brow, with hair pulled slightly off the face. These hats go well with off the shoulder, or shirtwaist styled gowns.

A *Tiara* crown is usually inset with pearls, gemstones, rhinestones, or crystals. It sits toward the front of the head and suits princess and bouffant styles best. This piece doesn't look attractive on short, straight hairstyles.

Wreaths are a circular band of fresh, or silk flowers. The flowers are often interwoven among pearls and lace, or you might have tulle or ribbon streamers cascading from the piece. The hatpiece sits on the crown, and compliments any dress style. Not for very short hairstyles.

WILL YOU WEAR A VEIL?

That will depend on the style of cap or headpiece you have chosen. Generally, the larger the hat, the shorter the veil. In addition, the more formal your wedding gown, the longer the veil can be. You have to make a few other decisions. Will you wear a single or multi-layer veil? A blusher veil? (Worn over your face in the procession, moved back during the ceremony). Most veils have lace or rolled edges, some embroidery design, and possibly seed pearls and other ornamentation. Make sure it matches your gown! Some veils can be made detachable from the cap. If you choose that option you can enjoy your veil at the ceremony, then detach it for freer movement during the reception.

The most common veil lengths are pouf (small gathered tuft attached to back of headpiece), to the shoulder, elbow, fingertip, knees, or ankle (waltz). See illustrations for further details. If your dress is just knee length, your veil will look best if it's no longer than your chin.

Accessories—The Finishing Touches

What jewelry looks best with your gown? Should you wear gloves? What kind of shoes and hosiery? Will you have a special garter? Carry a ruffled parasol? Here are a few suggestions to consider:

Gloves should blend with the fabric and ornamentation of your gown to enhance the overall look. The only time they must be worn is for a very formal wedding. Otherwise, they are entirely optional. In summer, wear those of cotton or crochet. In winter, select stretch satin, taffeta, or kid leather. Any time of year is perfect for delicate lace. They look especially attractive with a Victorian style gown. If you're wearing a more sophisticated design, select shimmery gloves with nylon and lycra. Length is measured by buttons. A one-button stops at the wrist, and would be worn with a long-sleeve dress. Those with sixteen-buttons cover the entire arm. They look best with a sleeveless gown. If you will wear longer gloves, you can have the ring finger slit for easy removal at the ceremony. That's much simpler than trying to remove your whole glove at a time when your hands are probably shaking. Or select fingerless gloves (gauntlets).

Shoes should match the style and color of your dress. They may be covered with richly ornamented fabrics; or topped with satin rosettes, jewels, bows, sequins, or rhinestones. Wear pumps with a long, sweeping train. Heels would look attractive with a knee length gown. Don't forget to consider the ceremony location. An outdoor wedding is no place for spike heels—they'll sink into the grass. Start shopping after you choose your dress to allow plenty of time to find the right pair. Make sure they're comfortable—it will be a long day. In fact, it's best to shop for them in the afternoon when your feet are already a bit swollen. Naturally you'll want to break them in before the wedding. Make sure you wear them enough to get the bottoms scuffed. That will help prevent slippage. Of course these shoes should be worn to your final dress fitting so the hem length will be perfect.

Make sure you have the right *lingerie*. It should be a color that won't show through your dress. Be careful not to buy a slip that's too full for your style of gown. That's a common mistake! Remember that a slim sheath requires a body-clinging liner. A stiff petticoat of tulle, organdy or taffeta works well with a fuller skirt. And the fullest styles should have a hooped slip to provide proper support. Your bra should be one that looks best with your dress, whether it needs an underwire, strapless, or halter-backed style. Select hose in a pattern or design that adds to the ensemble. Wear simple hose with an elaborate gown, ornate hose with a simple dress. Your best bet is very sheer, and if you can't find a matching color, nude always works. Buy the right size, you'll want to be comfortable. And don't forget a spare pair!

Traditionally many brides chose pearls as their wedding day jewelry. A pearl choker looks perfect with a sweetheart or portrait neckline. If you have a low-backed dress, try trailing a long strand down your back. A simple locket or gold chain beautifully compliments most dresses. A brooch or locket with a velvet neck ribbon will look perfect with a Victorian gown. A simple bodice can be dressed up with a rhinestone pendant twisted together with a sixteen inch strand of pearls. Or combine elements in your gown's ornamentation in your jewelry—sequins, crystals, beads, tassels.

Choose earrings that are the right proportion for your headpiece and hairstyle. Drop earrings look best with a simple headpiece and upswept hair. An ornate headpiece is complimented by simple, button style earrings. For a more modern, sophisticated look, don't be afraid to wear colored gemstones, rubies, colored diamonds, sapphires. The important thing is to make sure your accessories won't steal attention from your gown.

Final touches might include a fur muff in winter, a ruffled satin parasol to top off a Victorian gown, an embroidered shawl, lace hankie, or a crocheted fan. A bible or prayerbook with a cover of rich lace, embroidery, or flowers always looks lovely. Don't forget the traditional Something Old, Something New, Something Borrowed, Something Blue! Many brides work these into their accessories, adding lace from their mother's wedding gown, a blue ribbon to their garter.

A handbag to carry your personal items should match your dress color. Be sure you have makeup, perfume, mirror, comb, kleenex, aspirin, safety pins, needle and thread, and spare nylons inside.

MAKING UP FOR YOUR WEDDING

Many brides choose to have their makeup professionally done on their wedding day. Whatever you do, don't try anything new (like a facial) right before the wedding. This is no time to discover you are allergic to something! If you prefer to do your own, here are a few tips for best results.

Keep it low-key and natural looking. Experiment beforehand wearing a blouse or towel the same color as your gown (stark-white, off-white, beige, ivory). Choose a foundation that blends well, you don't want a tell-tale line! Many experts recommend using a shade lighter than your usual one. Remember that the camera will intensify makeup mistakes.

If you are wearing white, pale beige, or yellow, choose a *foundation* that has slightly pink undertones. If your face is naturally red, use one with green tones. Matte foundation will absorb light and not reflect it off your skin.

Use a matte *powder* finish to prevent an oily glare. If your skin is very oily, try applying loose powder with your fingers for best results. Apply *blusher* subtly to the cheekbones, temples, and bridge of your nose. Avoid using orange tints, use a pink or plum shade.

Don't outline your *eyes* in a dark color—it will look overly dramatic in pictures. Select a clear shade that blends or compliments your eyeshadow. Try to avoid dark grey, or light pastel shades, they don't look as attractive in pictures. If you want to wear a colored *mascara,* apply a coat of black or brown first for a great overall look. Flick the colored wand over your lashes before it's totally dry. For best results—use waterproof mascara, it's going to be an emotional day.

For long lasting color, powder your lips before applying *lipstick.* Brown or orange shades will look faded in pictures, so choose plums or pinks. To create the illusion of full lips, use glossy, or frosted light shades. Flatter a full mouth with creamy colors. Dab a touch of gloss in the center of the lips for extra shimmer.

PRESERVING YOUR GOWN AND VEIL

Have your dress professionally dry cleaned. Even if it's not visibly soiled, the oils and moisture from your body will affect the material. The cleaner should not add starch or sizing to the dress—that can attract bugs that will damage it. After it is cleaned, let the fabric air until you can no longer smell the cleaning fluid. Then stuff the sleeves and any bouffant parts with acid-free tissue paper. (Acid will turn a dress yellow). Hang the dress on a padded, unscented hanger that has been wrapped in muslin. Never use a wire hanger or store it in a plastic bag from the cleaners. Even the air tight boxes many cleaners use are not the best storage material. Make a bag or wrap of unbleached cotton muslin (wash it in hot water several times first) and store your gown in that.

Remove your veil from the headpiece, and repair any damage before you wash it. Remember that the ornamentation is delicate, handle with care. Baste the veil to a piece of 100% cotton muslin (that was pre-washed in hot water and well rinsed). This will provide support for the veil. Put about three inches of lukewarm water in your bathtub, mix in a soapless detergent. Carefully lay your veil and use your hand to gently pat the fabric and work the suds through the fibers. Do not rub, wring, or twist any part of the veiling. Let the veil (and backing) lie in the tub while you drain the water, and as you gently refill it with lukewarm rinse water.

It will require at least three rinses to get the veil completely free of suds. When the water has rinsed clear, leave the veil and muslin in the tub and press it with a white (or ivory if your veil is that color) bath towel to squeeze out excess moisture. Lift out of the tub and layer on another large towel of matching color. Place a third matching towel on top of the veil and gently press out as much water as you can. Don't roll the towels. Leave them flat.

Once you have pressed out all the moisture, lay the veil and muslin piece on a fresh towel in front of a breezy window. Don't set it outside or in direct sunlight. When completely dry, roll the piece (veil side out) and cover with acid-free paper. Store in a bag similar to the one used for your dress.

Do not seal either bag with sticky tape or pins—they will eventually damage the fabric. For best results, baste the bag shut (don't catch any material).

Choosing Attire for the Female Attendants

Naturally you want your attendants dressed in attractive gowns that match the style of your wedding. Since they pay for their attire, it's only fair that they be given a voice in the selection. Your best bet is to shop ahead of time and select three or four gowns that you like. Ask the saleswoman to show only those dresses, then bring your attendants in to make the final decision. (Your choices can be spread out over several shops). This method will also avoid arguments among the attendants.

When you select the dresses, try to imagine the style on each girl. Will it suit her shape? Can she wear it again? Will she have to purchase special undergarments to wear with it? Do you like the colors? Is it reasonably priced? Don't forget the headpiece. Make sure it looks pretty on each —and is suitable for their hairstyles.

Ideally you will all gather together and select the items at the same time. It's a nice way for everyone to meet, and a good opportunity to discuss other details. Do you want them to wear a certain style of shoe? Should they be dyed to match the gowns? (Be sure to obtain swatches). Do you want them to wear jewelry? Must it match? What about gloves?

If an attendant lives out of town, bring along an instant camera and snap a photo of someone wearing the gown and headpiece so she can see the ensemble. Ask your salesperson for the style number, color number, name and phone number of manufacturer for both the dress and headpiece. Your attendant can take it to a bridal shop in her own town, be measured, and order the gown there. This makes it possible for her to obtain the proper number of fittings. Or shop at a national chain so that she can obtain everything at long distance quite easily. Make her feel a part of the plans by keeping her aware of what's going on.

Everyone's Guide to Wedding Apparel

The size of the wedding, time of day, location, and formality of your gown determine what everyone else will wear. Here is a general guide to attire, but it is always subject to changes in fashion and personal preferences.

TYPE	BRIDE	ATTENDANTS	MOTHERS
Formal Daytime	White, ivory, or light pastel. Floor length dresses, train, long gloves with short sleeve gowns, otherwise optional. Matching shoes, accessories.	Floor, ankle, or tea-length gowns, headpiece with or without short veil. Gloves optional, shoes match/blend. Their gowns should complement in style, color and length.	Floor length or 3/4 length dresses of simple style, small hats optional, matching accessories.
Formal Evening	After 6 p.m. Dress same as morning but fabric is more elaborate, more ornaments.	Long or ankle length evening dresses, elaborate fabric. Accessories same as day.	Floor or ankle length gowns, small head coverings, dressy accessories.
Semi-Formal	White or pastel in ankle or floor length. Veil no longer than elbow. Rest same as formal. Evening wedding has more elaborate fabric, trim.	Same as for formal but with simpler style and fabric.	Same as for formal wedding.
Informal	Floor, ankle or tea length Short veil or bridal hat. Matching accessories.	Same length dress as bride, however don't have to wear floor length if bride does. Simple, matching accessories.	Street length or suit, ensemble.
GUESTS	At a formal wedding women wear street-length dresses or suits during the day; floor, ankle, or tea-length gowns in the evening. Male's attire is co-ordinated with his escort, unless otherwise stated for the occasion. The most standard is a suit appropriate to the season.		

Men's Formalwear

The type of clothing that the groom and male members of the wedding party will wear depends upon the style of your wedding (see **Wedding Styles**) and the time of day and year. Two charts at the end of the chapter detail the traditional guidelines for what men should wear and when.

For any formal wedding, it's a common practice for all the men in the wedding party (including both fathers) to rent formal clothes for the day. These suits should be obtained from the same shop so that all the attire matches exactly.

Should you accompany your fiance? That depends on both your attitudes and personal preferences. Most grooms are at a loss in selecting formalwear, so you will probably be involved to some degree.

A good clue to the professionalism of the store personnel is the way the area is maintained. If it's neat, clean, and orderly, it's likely that the clothing you rent will be well-cared for. Remember, quality and service can be as important as price. They should carry nationally known labels (the ones you see in the bridal magazine ads). Inferior quality apparel look worn after just a few rentals. The accuracy of the measurements taken are also important, because the key to attractive looking formalwear is a proper fit. The most expensive tuxedo in the shop won't look like it, unless it's pressed and fitted properly.

Ideally, the groom should visit several shops and try on appealing styles. The shop employee should be trained to suggest the proper styles for your particular type of wedding. For best results, do the initial shopping about six months before the wedding if you're getting married during Spring or peak Summer (If not six months—at least four months before).

If you won't be accompanying him, make sure he has a description of the style and color of your gown and the bridesmaids dresses. The men's formalwear is supposed to compliment the ladies gowns. Ideally, give him swatches of the material for a perfect match. For example: If your gown is ivory or off-white, his formalwear should never be stark white.

FORMALWEAR STYLES

The final look of the ensemble is determined by the cut of the coat and it's lapels, type of shirt, neckwear, and vest or cummerbund; as well as the fabric of the clothing and the colors in the outfit. For example: Tailcoat, striped trousers, white wing collar shirt, cummerbund, and bow tie offer a formal look. Gray slacks, vest, and white shirt with turned down collar, black four-in-hand tie, and dinner jacket present a more informal effect.

Dinner Jacket

Double-Breasted

Classic

Cutaway

Full Dress Coattail

DAYTIME WEDDING

	Very Formal	Formal	Semi-Formal	Informal
Coat	Cutaway, long jacket, stroller. Black or grey.	Cutaway, stroller, tuxedo. Black, grey, dark blue, white: May-Sept.	Stroller, tuxedo, dinner jacket, suit. Black, grey, navy, white: May to Sept.	Business suit, blazer & slacks. Black, grey, navy, dark blue, white.
Trousers	Match or contrast jacket with classic side stripe.	Match or contrast jacket with classic side stripe.	Match jacket or co-ordinating color. Can have side stripe.	Match jacket or co-ordinating color.
Shirt	White, wing collar, French cuffs, studs.	White, with wing or fold down collar, French cuffs.	White or co-ordinating color, fold down collar.	Dress shirt of white or coordinate color.
Vest	Grey or black	Match slacks/tie	Match slacks/tie	Usually not worn.
Cummerbd	Grey or black	Match tie	Match tie if worn.	Usually not worn.
Tie	Ascot, or striped four-in-hand tie.	Ascot, bow tie, or four-in-hand.	Bow tie or four-in-hand.	Four-in-hand if worn.
Jewelry	Stickpin with ascot, cuff links, studs.	Stickpin, studs, cuff links.	Cuff links and/or studs.	As necessary.
Shoes	Black dress or white: May to Sept.	Black dress or white: May to Sept	Dress, as appropriate to attire.	As appropriate.
Hat/Gloves	Grey	Grey	Usually not worn.	Usually not worn.
Overcoat	Black or grey	Black or grey	Dark color	Dark color

EVENING WEDDING (CEREMONY AFTER 6 P.M.)

	Very Formal	Formal	Semi-Formal	Informal
Coat	Black tailcoat	Tuxedo Black, grey, white: May to Sept	Tuxedo, Dinner Jacket, Suit, Blazer. Black, grey, navy, white: May to Sept.	Business Suit, Blazer & Slacks, Black, grey, navy dark blue, white.
Trousers	Black with classic side stripe.	Match jacket with classic side stripe.	Match jacket or co-ordinating color. Can have side stripe. White slacks & dk blzr good for May to Sept.	Match jacket or co-ordinating color.
Shirt	White wing collar, French cuffs, studs.	White, with wing or fold down collar. French cuffs.	White or co-ordinating color, fold down collar.	Dress shirt of white or co-ordinating color.
Vest	White	Black or white.	Match slacks/tie	Match slacks if worn
Cummerbd	White	Black or white.	Match tie if worn.	Not worn.
Tie	White bow tie.	Ascot, bow tie, or four-in-hand.	Bow tie or four-in-hand.	Four-in-hand if worn.
Jewelry	Cuff links, studs.	Stickpin, studs, cuff links.	Cuff links and/or studs.	As necessary.
Shoes	Black patent dress	Black dress, white: May to Sept	Black dress, white: May to Sept	As appropriate.
Hat/Gloves	Black top hat. White gloves.	Black top hat. Grey or white gloves.	Usually not worn.	Not worn.
Overcoat	Black or grey.	Black or grey.	Dark color.	Dark color.

Flowers

Your floral arrangements form an attractive backdrop for your wedding, and contribute to the day's festive atmosphere. Whether they're serene and simple, or a cheerful pot-pourri of colors, your flowers create the mood.

WHERE TO FIND THEM

Generally a florist, private garden, or craft shop are your best sources. Most couples utilize the services of a florist. An experienced and reputable one can design arrangements suitable to both budget and personal style. In most cases, the florist handles everything from ordering and arranging the flowers to their delivery.

Although not appropriate for very formal weddings, silk flowers purchased from craft shops look realistic. They also have the advantage of keeping nicely long after the wedding is over. However, they can sometimes be more expensive than real flowers, and careful planning and comparisons should be made when selecting them. And remember, someone with time and talent must arrange the flowers.

CHOOSING THE FLORIST

Select a florist early. Many limit the number of weddings they will handle on a certain day, and the best will be booked first. Familiarize yourself with types of flowers and arrangements. You can visit any shop without an appointment, and browse through their catalogs to obtain ideas. Look through bridal magazines and books about flowers. What do you like or dislike? Are you attracted to simple or elaborate arrangements? Bright colors or cool tones? Are you put off by flowers with large heads? Make an appointment so you can receive personalized attention. Bring along pictures of the flowers and arrangements you like best. You'll also need to provide details about the time, place, and style of your wedding and attire. Have color swatches from the gowns with you for proper matching of ribbons and trim.

Your florist should provide design expertise that will translate your vision into beautiful arrangements. As you talk about your ideas and budget, keep an open mind to their suggestions. Some will provide albums of weddings they have done, or of floral arrangements for you to examine and discuss. Others prefer to draw sketches of their ideas. Inspect their work, and note the care they take with arrangements. Ask yourself:

- [ ] Do you like the work you see?
- [ ] Is it creative? Attractive?
- [ ] Is each flower head carefully arranged and wired?
- [ ] Do they seem to use too many fillers and greens?
- [ ] Place the stems in water-filled tubes?
- [ ] Do they seem to know what you want?
- [ ] Do they provide pew markers, canopies, trellises, aisle carpets, candles, and other accessories?
- [ ] Will they deliver and set up?

COST

Pricing is mainly determined by the season, number of arrangements, how intricate they are, and the types of flowers used in them. Individual blossoms vary in cost that is based on ease of production; availability, and the number of areas they grow in. As a rule; carnations are inexpensive, roses are high-priced, and orchids exorbitant. To keep costs down, put them together in small, simple designs that have only two or three kinds of colors and blooms. If money's no object, you can select a large, complex formation of ten different flowers in as many colors.

WHAT TO ORDER

Here's a list of the flowers normally purchased for weddings:

Bridal Bouquet The most popular style is the cascade bouquet, with flowers trailing down in a v-shape from the central arrangement. Other favorites include: a round bouquet, single flower, a floral covered prayer book, or a spray of long-stemmed roses held in the arm.

White flowers are primarily used in the traditional arrangements, with a combination of roses, orchids, stephonitas, and baby's breath. Daisies, lilies of the valley, and carnations are also used in many bouquets. The most popular include white roses, orchids, gardenias, and lilies of the valley.

Bride's Throw-Away Bouquet Some brides toss the flowers they've carried all day during the appropriate moment of the reception. Others prefer to keep that arrangement for sentimental reasons, and toss either a detachable section (pre-arrange to have it made this way) or a small bouquet prepared especially for this custom.

Bride's Going Away Corsage If and when you change into regular clothes at the end of the reception, it's customary in some areas for the groom to present you with a corsage.

Female Attendants The bridesmaids, maid of honor, and flower girl all carry flowers, and sometimes wear them in their hair.

Groom He wears a boutonniere, usually made of a few flowers of the type in your bouquet.

Male Attendants The best man, groomsmen, ushers, fathers of the bride and groom, ringbearers, and pages wear boutonnieres. They're usually of white carnations or roses. The best man may have a slightly different variety to set him off from the others. If the men wear handkerchiefs in their breast pocket, or military uniforms, they wouldn't wear boutonnieres.

Mothers Wear a corsage of orchids or roses made to match or complement their dress color.

Grandparents, Godparents In some areas, it's customary for the women to receive simple white corsages. The men wear boutonnieres of white carnations or roses. This purchase is optional.

Ceremony Site If you marry in a church, order at least one arrangement for each side of the altar. A trellis (arch of flowers) or other arrangements can be used to decorate the site. In Roman Catholic ceremonies, there are also flowers for Mary's Shrine.

Reception Site There are usually centerpieces or floral arrangements for the head table, dining tables, refreshment table, cake and buffet tables.

Other Occasions Corsages for the engagement party, showers, and the rehearsal and its' dinner are supplied by the groom. (He may not be aware of this custom).

KINDS OF FLOWERS TO USE

Your florist should be an expert on all types of flowers, their availability, stamina, and cost. He can suggest appropriate substitutes when necessary.

Most, especially those popular for weddings, are available through your florist year-round. For best results select those that bloom during your wedding season. They are not only less expensive, they have larger blooms and healthier stems. Here is a guide to most popular flowers, by season:

FLOWER NAME	DESCRIPTION	SPRING	SUMMER	FALL	WINTER	ALL YEAR
Amaryllis	Long stem, lily shape, white or red.	X			X	
Anemone	Large, poppy shape, many colors.	X	X	X		
Aster	Also known as Michaelmas Daisies.	X	X			
Autumn Crocus	Unusual leaves, white, purple flowers.			X		
Baby's Breath	Tiny, lacy, usually white, some red.					X
Bachelor Button	Small, carnation-shaped, many colors.		X	X		
Calla Lily	Usually white, lovely shape.			X	X	
Carnations	Very fragrant, many colors.					X
Chrysanthemum	Many shapes, colors, sizes.			X	X	
Cosmos	Daisy shape, feathery foliage.		X			
Crocus	Usually bright yellow.	X				
Daffodil	White, orange, yellow, bi-color.	X				
Daisy	Usually white with yellow center.		X	X		
Day Lily	Many stem lengths, colors.	X	X	X		
Delphinium	Long spikes, lacy foliage, many colors.	X	X	X		
Forget Me Not	Dainty blue with white or yellow centers.	X				
Foxglove	Long spikes, trumpet-shape flowers.		X			
Gardenia	Fragrant white with dark leaves.	X				
Iris	Long stalks, large petals.	X	X	X		
Lilac	Tiny lavender or white flowers.	X				
Lily	Many varieties, colors.	X	X			
Lily of Valley	Long spikes, clusters of white flowers.	X				
Orchid	Mostly white, lavender, expensive.					X
Peony	Wide flower, cream, white, red.		X			

FLOWER NAME	DESCRIPTION	SPRING	SUMMER	FALL	WINTER	ALL YEAR
Rain Lily	(Zephyr) smaller than most lilies.		X	X		
Rose	Many varieties, colors, sizes.					X
Spray Orchid	Spikes with tiny orchid shape flowers.				X	
Stephonitas	White trumpet-shape flowers.		X			
Strawflower	Daisy shape, straw-like petals.		X			
Tulip	Familiar petal shape, many colors.	X				
Violet	Tiny, fragrant, blue, white, purple.	X				
Zephyr Lily	Small lilies in white, yellow, pink.			X	X	

SELECTING YOUR ARRANGEMENTS

The mixture of colors used in an arrangement, along with the size and shape of the flowers and their placement, provides the overall effect of warmth or coolness. Warm colors, such as red, orange, and yellow, pull the eye to them and attract attention from a distance. Cool colors, such as blue, purple, and lavender, move away from the eye and stay in the background. Every arrangement also has an accent color to pull the scheme together. The amount of accent color you use depends on the affect you want. Here is a good way to see how colors work:

Imagine an arrangement with white, orange, and gold flowers. Add a few bright crimson to the picture—see the difference? Take away the crimson and use kelly green. Again, see the change in perspective one color can make?

You want the colors in your arrangement to harmonize. Those too near one another on the color wheel will blend each other out. The most severe contrast comes from colors farthest apart on the color wheel. Consider the deep and startling affect of using a combination of bright reds and yellows. On the other hand, a pale blue and pale yellow would produce a soft, gentle, impression. A dark, deep blue with a pastel yellow would present a broken design. For total harmony, select one hue and its' tints—yellow, dark yellow, and pale yellow.

What light will your flowers be seen in? Warm colors are dulled by shade or shadow. The advancing and receding of your color combinations, either in blending them or contrasting them, are what gives the arrangements their beautiful affects.

Simple arrangements using only white flowers add to the formality of the wedding. For a more informal ceremony, combine pastel colors: pale blue, cream, ice pink, peach, and lilac.

Bridal Registries

It's popular for couples to register their gift preferences after setting the wedding date. Many larger department stores and some discount outlets offer this service. You and your fiance choose items you'd like to have in your new home. The store records your selections in their computer. Any guest who wishes to use the registry receives a copy of your wish list, and if they purchase an item on the list the store shows that gift has been purchased on future printouts. That way you avoid duplicate gifts.

Register at a store that has a variety of items you find attractive, and is convenient to most of your friends and family. If that particular store has branches, they will update your registry throughout all the stores. If you register at more than one, don't list the same items! That defeats the purpose of the registry and you'll receive duplicate gifts. Try to avoid picking a large number of high-ticket items. Too many couples justify these choices by saying "People can group together to buy these." People don't do that very often, and you'll end up with a lot of gifts that weren't from your registry as substitutes.

This system gives you an opportunity to look at items and make selections. It's also a discreet way to let others know what you'd like to have.

Naturally, guests don't have to use a registry, but many prefer it to trying to second-guess your preferences or what you currently own. While the registry can be used for any gifts given the two of you, it's primarily used for shower and wedding presents. Guests can learn where you are registered by asking family members and wedding attendants. Shower invitations should also include a listing of where you are registered. Here are some items you might list:

☐ China	☐ Glassware
☐ Casserole Dishes	☐ Kitchen Utensils
☐ Food Processor	☐ Cannisters
☐ Cutlery	☐ Coffee Pot
☐ Baking Pans	☐ Spice Rack
☐ Electric Skillet	☐ Jello Molds
☐ Mixing Bowls	☐ Salad Bowls
☐ Tea Kettle	☐ Stainless Flatware
☐ Serving Trays	☐ Pots and Pans
☐ Napkin Rings	☐ Knife Sharpener
☐ Toaster	☐ Can Opener
☐ Mixer	☐ Microwave
☐ Iron	☐ Ironing Board
☐ Candlestick Holders	☐ Vacuum Cleaner
☐ Scale	☐ Cutting Board
☐ Bath Towels	☐ Kitchen Towels
☐ Tablecloths	☐ Napkins
☐ Place Mats	☐ Crystal
☐ Dessert Dishes	☐ Coffeemaker
☐ Paintings	☐ Sheets
☐ Blankets	☐ Bedspread
☐ Pillows	☐ Clothes Hamper
☐ Throw Rugs	☐ Shelving Unit
☐ Entertainment Center	☐ Clocks
☐ Wall Hangings	☐ Figurines
☐ Furniture	☐ Television
☐ Stereo	☐ Luggage

Gifts

A part of the wedding tradition is the giving and receiving of gifts. This celebration marks a rite of passage, and is important to both the family and community. Guests invited to showers and the reception will present them to you and your fiancee. You and your fiance will in turn give gifts to each other, your attendants, and to any other people who offered special help during the planning or on your wedding day.

What You'll Receive

Some gifts will arrive before the wedding. Traditionally, these are put on display at your parent's home until one week after the wedding. Ideally, guests won't bring gifts to the reception, but it does happen. Don't open them there. It makes it awkward for those who sent their gifts in advance. If you wish to exhibit them at the reception, hire extra security. However, such a display might embarrass guests who could only afford modest gifts. Here are the most popular wedding presents:

1. Money
2. Silver serving dishes, vases, candlesticks, accessories
3. Crystal vases, bowls, accessories
4. Silverware/Flatware
5. Tableware (dishes)
6. Cookware (pots and pans)
7. Sheets, blankets, towels
8. Lamps
9. Vacuum Cleaner
10. Blender/Food Processor, or small appliances

Someone (usually the bride or her mother) needs to maintain a record of the gifts and their donors for easy reference when writing thank you notes. Although most gifts are returnable, it's a good idea to keep as many as possible to avoid hurt feelings.

Naturally, a thank you note should be written for each gift. It's fairly common today for the groom to help write them. These notes should be sent out within a reasonable period of time, no later than one month after the wedding. Pre-addressing them before the wedding makes this task easier. If you are having difficulties with this bothersome but necessary job, may I suggest the *Bride's Thank You Guide: Thank You Writing Made Easy*. It's packed with dozens of sample letters designed to save you loads of time and effort.

GIFTS THAT YOU GIVE

It's best to present your groom with a personal momento. Something he'll treasure always with sentimental value to symbolize your future together. This isn't a good time to be practical and get him a new set of tires. Traditionally, it's a gift of jewelry, such as a fine, engraved watch. Give it to him shortly before the wedding, perhaps after the wedding rehearsal. Here are some additional ideas:

- Pearl, Diamond (or other jewel) tie pin.
- A very, very expensive bottle of cologne.
- Music box that plays 'your song' or something that was played during the ceremony.

Attendants should receive their gifts at the bride's luncheon or rehearsal dinners. It's traditional to provide identical items to each, although the maid of honor should receive something extra special. The flower girl might need a gift that's a little less sophisticated than the others. It's nice to personalize the items with your name and wedding date if possible. If you have a special hobby or talent, you may wish to make each person a special momento. Here are some ideas:

- Necklace
- Bracelet
- Locket
- Earrings

- Decorative hair comb
- Key ring
- Expensive compact
- Pen set
- Jewelry box
- Charm
- Pin
- Calculator
- Pictures from the wedding
- Personalized stationery
- Desk accessories set

- Purse
- Perfume
- Music Box
- Engraved letter opener
- Earring box
- Ornate belt
- Wallet
- Photo frame
- Business card holder
- Desk nameplates
- Miniature tape recorder

Anyone who provided special help during the planning, or on your wedding day should also receive a gift. This includes friends who might have sung, performed or assisted at your wedding and refused payment. In addition, your parents, the groom's parents, and anyone who contributed financially to the wedding should receive flowers afterwards with an appreciative note.

Invitations

An invitation card is sent to ask friends and family to join your celebration, and to provide them with information. Unlike the casual invitation most of us are accustomed to receiving, the wedding invite has a format of it's own. The type of invitation you send will provide your guest with a clue to what kind of wedding you're having. A richly engraved bid on thick white or cream paper signals an elegant, formal occasion. A personal note written on stationery implies a small, informal affair.

Wedding invitations can be selected through large sample catalogs available in wedding shops, department stores that carry wedding attire, florists, photographers, print shops, and any other retail shop that deals with the wedding trade. They're also available through mail order catalogs which offer the convenience of choosing your invitations in the comfort of your own home. Their names and addresses can be found in bridal magazines. They'll send a free catalog of samples if you write and ask for them.

There are many types and styles to choose from. Some are plain or have a simple border design. Others have elaborate artwork embossed with gold or silver foil. You can select colors ranging from ivory to lavender, styles that include your engagement photograph on them, and paper from very thin parchment to very thick vellum. In addition, you pick the type and size of the lettering on the invitations, and the color of the ink.

Wedding invitations are almost always issued by the bride's parents, even if they didn't contribute to the expenses. An older bride (especially one who has been married before) might wish to issue the invitation in her and her fiance's name, but it's not necessary. If circumstances won't allow the bride's parents to be the hosts, the invitations can be issued by a guardian, friend, or the bride and groom. Sometimes the the groom's parents are included on the invitation, but that's entirely optional.

If you are having a very formal wedding, your invitation should be the traditional style. That's a cream or ivory bid with a simple border. The words are printed on the front (the inside is blank). The paper is of thick quality, and the wording is engraved with black ink.

Engraved script is very proper and traditional, but it's also an expensive process. It's now used only for very formal weddings, or by those who can easily afford it. Most couples choose a thermo-engraving process which offers the raised appearance of engraved letters at a much better price.

WHAT TO ORDER

Besides the actual invitation to the wedding ceremony, there are several separate cards made of matching stationery ordered and included in the invitation mailing.

- A reception card offers the details about the reception. This is especially important if there are guests invited to the ceremony who won't be invited to the reception.
- Response cards are the best way to discover how many people will attend the reception. This is important if you'll have a catered dinner, because the number of guests the caterer prepares for directly affects the size of his bill. They're enclosed in envelopes pre-addressed by the printer (usually to the bride's parent's home) and a stamp is often placed on the envelope for convenience (optional). The card has a place for the person to write his or her name, and the number of persons from that family that will attend. Guests are asked to respond before a certain date (a few days before the caterer's deadline). The guests only need to complete the card, seal the envelope, and drop it in the mail.
- Some stationers offer Response Postcards, which do the same job, but without the envelope. Because postal rates are less expensive for postcards, this is a cost-cutting option if you plan to pre-stamp the response cards you send to your guests.
- If you know your new address you can include cards that contain that information. Called 'At Home' cards, they usually include the effective date.
- Pew cards are used at more formal weddings. They're placed inside invitations to those who will be seated in the special reserved section called "in the ribbons". This would include honored guests, grandparents, godparents, siblings, or whomever you wish to seat there. Seating in this section is very limited. If you're concerned about security at the ceremony, pew cards can be enclosed with each invitation, with the instruction to present it to the usher for admittance.

The invitations should be ordered about three months before the wedding. You need to allow for the printing process, checking and correcting any errors, and time to address and mail them six weeks before the wedding.

WORDING

There are customary guidelines for wording your invitations. Many varieties are used, but the more formal your wedding, the closer to tradition yours should be. Note that the words honour and favour are always spelled with 'our' on wedding stationery. The words 'honour of your presence' usually appear in invitations to church ceremonies; the words 'pleasure of your company' appear on invitations to non-church ceremonies and wedding receptions.

WEDDING INVITATION

Traditional invitation from bride's parents.

Mr. and Mrs. James Walsh
request the honour of your presence
at the marriage of their daughter
Jillian Marie
to
Mr. Daniel Robert Hernandez
Saturday, the 26th of August
one-thousand nine-hundred and ninety-five
at four o'clock
First United Church
74 West 86th Street
New York, New York

Bride's Mother Widowed

Mrs. Charles Wang
requests the honour of your presence
at the marriage of her daughter
Karen Lynn
to
Mr. Jeffrey Allen Grady
Sunday, the fourth of January
one-thousand nine-hundred and ninety-five
at six o'clock in the evening
Church of God
23 Roanoke Avenue
Farmington, Massachusetts

Both bride's parents divorced and remarried.
Issued by her parents alone.

Your mom's name always goes first:

Mrs. Michael Davidson
and
Mr. Richard P. Goldman
request the pleasure of your company
at the marriage of their daughter
Sarah Elizabeth
to
Mr. Michael Wayne Klimczyk
on Saturday, the seventh of June
one-thousand nine-hundred and ninety-five
at three o'clock in the afternoon
Hyatt Park Pavilion
2880 Spruce Street
Grosse Pointe, Michigan

Both bride's parents divorced and remarried.
Issued to include step-parents.

Your mom's name always goes first:

Mr. and Mrs. Roger McNaughton
and
Mr. and Mrs. Kevin P. Felton
request the pleasure of your company
at the marriage of their daughter
Jennifer Marie
to
Mr. Joshua David McCabe
on Saturday, the seventh of June
one-thousand nine-hundred and ninety-five
at three o'clock in the afternoon
Hyatt Park Pavilion
2880 Spruce Street
Grosse Pointe, Michigan

Bride's step-mother and father are hosts.

Mr. and Mrs. Richard Dean
request the honour of your presence
at the marriage of Mrs. Dean's stepdaughter
Kelly Ann
to
Robert Stephen Victor
on Friday, the eighth of July
one-thousand nine-hundred and ninety-five
at one o'clock in the afternoon
First Methodist Church

Issued by both the bride and groom's parents.

Mr. and Mrs. Edward M. Curtis
request the honour of your presence
at the marriage of their daughter
Danielle Marie
to
Mr. Patrick Thomas Jacobson
son of Mr. and Mrs. James F. Jacobson
on Friday, the first of August
one-thousand nine-hundred and ninety-five
at four o'clock in the afternoon
St. Joseph's Church
Calvary Circle
Richmond, Indiana

By the groom's parents.

Mr. and Mrs. Jason Paul Smith
request the honour of your presence
at the marriage of Stacy Marie Vasquez
to their son
Mr. John Michael Smith
on Saturday, the ninth of September
one-thousand nine-hundred and ninety-five
at half past ten o'clock in the morning
Hope Lutheran Church
432 North River Drive
Tupelo, Mississippi

By the bride and groom

The honour of your presence
is requested at the marriage of
Lynnette Ellen Chung
to
David Michael Kumar
on Monday, the first of May
one-thousand nine-hundred and ninety-five
at two o'clock in the afternoon
St. Paul's Church
21 Garfield Street
Cleveland, Ohio

94

SMALL WEDDING, BIG RECEPTION

If you want a small, intimate gathering at your ceremony; but a large party for your reception, you would send invitations to the reception, and enclose a card for the ceremony (the reverse of tradition). Your invitations might read as follows:

Mr. & Mrs. Thomas Michael Christenson
request the pleasure of your company
at the wedding reception of their daughter
Rebecca Lynn
and
Mr. Phillip James Waterton
Saturday, the sixteenth of June
one-thousand nine-hundred and ninety-five
at half past six o'clock
Quail River Country Club
St. Paul, Minnesota

Ceremony cards would read:

Mr. & Mrs. Thomas Michael Christenson
request the honour of your presence
Saturday, the sixteenth of June
one-thousand nine-hundred and ninety-five
at half past five o'clock
United Presbyterian Church
St. Paul, Minnesota

MILITARY WEDDING

- If you or your groom are ranked Captain or above in the Army, (or Lieutenant Senior Grade or above in the Navy), your title appears before your name. (Captain Linda Wilson, United States Army)
- If ranked below, your title would be listed after your name. (Laura Johnson, Ensign, United States Navy).

SMALL, INFORMAL WEDDING

If there are less than fifty guests, a short, handwritten note from you or the hostess is sufficient. It might read something like this:

Dear Bob and Jennifer,
Laura and John will be married at 2 p.m Saturday, May
1st, at First Baptist Church , Main Street. A small
reception will follow at the Windsor Hotel. Please join us
for this happy occasion.

Love,
Linda and Phil

RECEPTION CARD

For formal weddings, or in situations where guests invited to the ceremony will not automatically be invited to the reception, you should enclose a card describing the details. It is issued in the name of the hosts of the wedding, the same names that issue the wedding invitation. It might read as follows:

Mr. and Mrs. Peter M. Silman
request the pleasure of your company .
on Saturday, the 23rd of March
at half after five o'clock in the evening
Sportsman's Club, 25 Deer Road, San Diego, California

Couples who prefer adults only at the reception could word it:

The pleasure of your company
is requested at a reception for adults
at five-thirty in the evening
Shelby Park Pavilion
200 Country Club Road
Laramie, Wyoming

If you will have the same guests at both the ceremony and reception, you can add the information on the bottom left-hand corner of the invitation. Wording might be:

Reception following the ceremony

OR

Reception at six o'clock
Briar Ridge Community Hall
63 Wilson Road
Kansas City, Kansas

RESPONSE CARD

You don't have to enclose a response card. In the bottom corner of the invitation you may state:

R.S.V.P. or Please Respond

---

followed by your mother's or your own address. However, since weddings are quite expensive, and so many people are lax in sending R. S. V. P.'s, most bride's feel it is worth the time and expense to enclose separate response cards to remind the guests that you definitely need to know if they are coming or not.

The cards match the wedding stationery, and are enclosed in envelopes pre-addressed by the printer. Although it's not required, the bride often places a stamp on them for the guest's convenience. The guest writes their name and the number attending on the card, seals the envelope, and drops it in the mailbox. A typical response card reads:

The favour of a reply is requested
before July 28, 1995

M_____

Number of Persons _____

> *Kindly respond by October 24, 1995*
>
> M_____
>
> *Number of Persons* _____

PEW CARD

Pew cards are not necessary unless you are having a very formal wedding, distinguished guests, or are concerned about uninvited guests and wish to control the entrance of all those attending the ceremony. The card your guest presents to the usher might read:

> *Please present this card*
> *at St. Patrick's Cathedral*
> *on Saturday, the 19th of July*

The pew number, or the words 'within the ribbons' can be indicated on the card when appropriate. Or you can write the person's name across the top.

AT HOME (NEW ADDRESS) CARDS

To notify friends and family of your new address, you can enclose a printed card with the following information:

> *Mr. and Mrs. Robert Stephen Smith*
>
> *after the ninth of September*
>
> *1411 Long Hill Drive, Denver, Colorado 76323*

These cards are also an ideal way to notify friends and family if you do not intend to adopt your husband's name. The top line could indicate the way you wish to be addressed after the wedding, such as:

> Ann Beckwith and Robert Stephen Smith
>
> Or
>
> Ann Beckwith-Smith and Robert Stephen Smith

CEREMONY PROGRAMS

It's not very expensive to have ceremony programs printed, and they make excellent souvenirs for your guests on your special day. You can find samples in invitation catalogs, through religious supply and stationery stores, and local printers. Most have pre-made covers and layouts, and you place your information in the proper locations. You want to be careful with the ones that include everything but your name and date. They usually include every possible option that might occur during the ceremony—which can confuse the guests even more.

Programs are especially helpful if your wedding service will be unfamiliar to many of the guests. You can include explanatory information, and note where they should join in. You don't have to include every detail of the ceremony. These should offer no more than the most pertinent information. The cover should be of whatever design appeals to you, as long as it suits the style of your wedding. Here's some information you might want to include in yours:

Inside Front

Worship Service
Celebrating the Marriage of
Pamela Ann Sullivan
and
Thomas Michael Wilson
Saint Anne's Church
Mackinac Island, Michigan
August 23, 1995
at
twelve o'clock noon

Rev. James Garfield
Officiating

Inner Pages

Prelude Music	Homily
Processional	Statement of Intentions
Opening Prayers	Vows
Solo: Ave Maria	Ring Ceremony
By: Florence Zonacky	Congregation Prayers
Scripture Reading	Solo
By: Linda Simpson	Lord's Prayer
Scripture Reading	Benediction/Blessing
By: Laura Gracine	Recessional

Inside Back

OUR WEDDING PARTY	Groomsmen
Maid of Honor	Ronald Wilson
Helen Wilson	Robert Sullivan
Best Man	Flower Girl
Randy Jackson	Cheryl Bentley
Bridesmaids	Ring Bearer
Karen Chung	Fred Thomas
Barb Sullivan	Vocal Soloist
Jennifer Paul	Jean Hernandez

You can also include: Your parent's names, and the names of anyone else who provided special music or services. A special greeting to your guests. A meaningful prayer. Your individual vows. Translations of any prayers spoken in another language. Details about a custom that will be a part of the ceremony.

The ushers can hand these out before the ceremony, or they can be placed in decorative baskets at the entrance. Be sure to print enough so that guests who couldn't make the ceremony can have them as souvenirs. Printing costs decrease with volume, so have a supply for the reception guests too.

WEDDING ANNOUNCEMENTS

Primarily used if you have a small wedding and reception. They are sent to all of the people that you would like to have invited, but weren't able to because of space or budget limitations. The announcements should be mailed after the wedding ceremony—have them addressed beforehand. Persons receiving an announcement are not obligated to purchase a gift. It is a nice way to provide them with details of this important change in your life, and a souvenir most will appreciate. Standard wording for announcements is:

Mr. and Mrs. William Dayton Milton
have the honour of announcing
the marriage of their daughter
Deborah Anne
and
Mr. Kevin Hunt Phillips
on Saturday, the fifth of May
One-thousand nine-hundred and ninety-three
Santa Fe, New Mexico

THANK YOU CARDS

Thank You stationery is available in two basic styles. The "Informal" is printed on paper matching your invitations and has your names printed on the front: "Mr. & Mrs. Donald P. Smith". Less formal are the cards that simply have "Thank You" printed on the front.

Take time to send each guest a handwritten note. Whether they sent a check, or spent hours selecting a gift, they deserve your personal acknowledgement. Pre-printed verses with your names printed on the bottom might save you time, but your guests, the people you cared about enough to invite to your celebration, deserve more than such an impersonal response.

Try to pre-address the envelopes to save time, and send out your notes as you receive each gift to avoid a backlog. Before the wedding sign your maiden name, after the wedding sign your married name. There's nothing wrong with your fiance helping out, and he can sign his name to any note he writes.

Your note should show gratitude, mention something noteworthy about the gift and how it might be used. For a gift of money, tell what you'll use it for. It's considered impolite to mention the amount.

Once again, if you need help in preparing the notes, I strongly recommend the *Bride's Thank You Guide*. Sample letters covering scores of different gifts and situations are a wonderful time saver.

PROOFREADING

It's important to carefully examine your invitation for errors. Ideally, your printer will present you with a sample several weeks before they are finished. Whatever the case, examine them carefully before you take them home. Here are a few items to watch for:

☐ Is this the right color paper?
☐ Does it have the correct weight and texture?
☐ Are they properly printed, or out of alignment?
☐ Is it the style you ordered?
☐ Is the wording exactly as you requested?
☐ Are the lines in the proper places?
☐ Is it the correct weekday, date, and year?
☐ Is the time correct? Is it written out in words (not numbers)?
☐ Are honour and favour spelled with a 'u'? (They should be).
☐ Are the ceremony and reception sites correct?
☐ Are the addresses correct?
☐ Are all the names spelled correctly?
☐ Are commas and apostrophes in the right places?
☐ Do the enclosure cards have the correct information?
☐ Do they match the rest of the stationery?
☐ Do response card envelopes have the correct address?

MAPS

If your wedding or reception is in an out of the way location, or if you have out of town guests, it's very helpful and appreciated if you supply maps. You can draw your own, obtain one from the local Chamber of Commerce, sketch your directions and photocopy it, or use any other map you can find. Be sure that the directions are clear and concise, and easy for someone unfamiliar with the area to understand. Turnoffs should be clearly marked, and it might help to note points to watch for in the margin. (Turn left on Harrison Road—just past the marina).

ADDRESSING

Wedding invitations should be addressed by hand. Both the inner and outer envelopes have a proper format, and all names are completely written out—no abbreviations. When two names are listed on the outer envelope, they appear in alphabetical order. Children under sixteen would have their names written on the inner envelope if they are invited. Anyone over sixteen should receive their own invitation. Here is a chart that details the proper form for addressing in various situations:

Guest	Inner Envelope	Outer Envelope
Married couple	Mr. & Mrs. Martin	Mr. & Mrs. John M. Martin
Wife kept maiden name	Ms. Carlson Mr. Martin	Ms. Barbara P. Carlson Mr. John M. Martin
Unmarried man	Mr. Jones and Guest	Mr. Thomas Jones
Unmarried woman	Ms. Andrews and Guest	Ms. Melissa Andrews
Engaged couple or Unmarried, live together	Mr. Babcock Ms. Felicity	Mr. James Babcock and Ms. Marguerite Felicity
Divorced woman	Ms. Hernandez	Ms. Anna Jones Hernandez
Widow	Ms. or Mrs. Wang	Mrs. David Wang or Ms. Helen Wang
Over 16, still at home	Miss or Ms. O'Hara Mr. Silverman	Miss or Ms. Jane O'Hara Mr. William Silverman

Be sure to have an accurate compilation of all names and addresses well before the time you sit down to write them. You don't want deliveries delayed—or worse yet returned to you because of inaccurate information. If you need a zip code-visit your local Post Office and look it up in the directory. Don't send an invitation without one.

Write clearly (never type them). Some brides hire professional calligraphers—but it's not necessary. Traditionally the ink color should be blue or black. Include your return address in the upper left corner, the Post Office frowns on those placed on the back flap.

ASSEMBLING

1. Put tissue over the wording of your invitations. (Originally meant to keep the ink from smearing, these are not necessary, but customary).
2. Place any enclosure cards and maps inside the invitation.
3. Place the invitation in the inner envelope fold-side down, with print side facing back flap.
4. Do not seal the inner envelope.
5. Put the inner envelope in the outer one. The front side (where you handwrote the names) should be facing the outer envelope's back flap.

MAILING

Ideally you will have assembled a sample invitation package before you ordered them, and had it weighed at the Post Office. You want to avoid having to place postage for more than one ounce on each envelope. Mail them four to six weeks before the wedding date.

WHAT'S IN A NAME?

Should you keep your maiden name...take your husband's last name...or combine the two? Every bride has to consider these options. For many years, it was customary for the bride to take her husband's last name as her own. This was always a tradition, never a law—except in a few States. Today, it's a personal decision.

Some brides choose to keep their maiden name for professional use, and their husband's name for social occasions. This can be confusing to some people. Keep credit records, legal documents, and other data such as your passport in just one of the names.

The best way to inform people that you'll be keeping your maiden name after your marriage is to enclose a card when you send your wedding announcements/invitations. It could read something like:

> *Sarah Johnson will retain her present name for*
> *all legal and social purposes after the marriage.*

Should you decide to hyphenate your names, put them in the order that sounds best. If you choose this alternative, you should both hyphenate your names. If you have children, they can either use the hyphenated name, or pick one of them to use.

If you are not following the tradition of adopting your husband's name, you may also want to include the correct information in the newspaper announcements of your marriage.

Sign your maiden name to any thank you written before the wedding, your married name to those written after the marriage took place. If you will change your name, don't forget to document that change on your driver's license, passport, insurance policy, and other important papers.

Guest List

Most people love to attend a wedding. It's an opportunity to celebrate a joyful event; and to take part in wishing the couple lifelong happiness. The number of invitations you send will be influenced by your budget, and the style of your wedding. Ideally, you should include all the people you would truly miss if they weren't there. It doesn't always work out that way.

Some people might assume they'll be invited. Don't let such assumptions upset your plans. No one has a right to an invitation. There are even people who might give you a gift before they've received an invitation. That doesn't mean you must add them to the guest list (although they do deserve a thank you note). When confronted with these and similar situations, just explain that because it will be a small wedding you cannot extend an invitation. You might suggest getting together for dinner at another time so they'll have a chance to share your happiness.

Everyone who will attend the wedding should receive an invitation; including parents, your clergyman, and members of the bridal party. These special participants don't need to reply formally, the invitations are a keepsake momento of the occasion. You don't have to allow your unmarried friends to bring a guest, especially if it's a very small wedding. However, if someone is engaged, or part of a well-established couple, their partner should be included if possible.

It's difficult to make plans until you have some idea of the number of guests that will be invited. As a rule, expect at least 75% of the guests you invite to attend. This number can vary during summer months, when vacations, other weddings, and activities may conflict with your date. If there have been a series of recent weddings or large gatherings in your family, attendance will decrease with each subsequent occasion. If the family hasn't gathered in a long time, a larger percentage may attend. All guests should be made aware as early as possible if your wedding will occur during the holiday season in order to plan accordingly—most people are very busy during that period.

The bride's family traditionally sets the size of the guest list and the groom's family receives half the allotted slots. it doesn't matter whose family has more relatives and friends. If two-hundred invitations will be sent, his family has the option of inviting one-hundred. (They can offer to return slots if they don't need them and your family does).

You, your fiance, and both mothers need to sit down and make tentative lists. Divide potential guests into three categories:

OPTIONAL	PROBABLE	DEFINITE

Put friends, relatives, neighbors, and co-workers under the appropriate category. It will make it much easier to cut the list if it becomes necessary. You'll probably move some names among the columns before finally deciding where they belong. Any people cut from your definite list should be sent wedding announcements. Consult telephone books, address books, and the necessary people for up to date addresses—and to make sure you haven't forgotten anyone! When all lists are complete, check for duplicates. You may be surprised to learn that your parents know some of the same people—we were!

An up-to-date and organized list can provide handy reference for wedding and shower invitations, as well as information for writing thank you notes. One handy system uses index cards, as shown in the sample below. You can purchase similar pre-printed cards in many stationery stores; or blank ones in any drug store and make them up yourself. To save time, keep the cards in alphabetical order.

GUEST ORGANIZER CARD

☐ Bride's Guest ☐ Groom's Guest		
Name:		
# of Persons:	Children/&Guest:	
Address:		
Phone #	Notes:	
SHOWER		
Invited:	Attended:	Thank You Sent:
Gift Received:		
WEDDING		
Invited:	R.S.V.P.:	# Attending:
Gift Received:		Thank You Sent:

At a glance you can learn:

1. If the invitation has been sent.
2. If the guest has responded to the invitation, and how.
3. How many guests are invited.
4. How many guests have accepted.
5. Necessary information to address invitations and write thank you notes.
6. Details about gifts for writing thank you notes.

Naturally these cards will also be useful for future correspondence after the wedding, or for forming guest lists for other family gatherings.

Ideally, all guests will respond by the date you request. In reality, it doesn't happen. A certain number will not respond, but show up. A few who responded positively may not be there because of last minute emergencies. A week or two before the wedding, discreetly inqure about the intention of guests who haven't responded. At the price of catering today, you don't want to pay for a lot of empty place settings.

Many factors can make the guest list grow. Here are a few to prepare for:

1. Most people understand that if you're having a small gathering of 75 people the guest list will be limited. But, if you're having 200, everyone develops the attitude of 'what's one more'. Suddenly, great aunt Millie wants to invite her neighbor, your mother her tennis club, and your father all his cronies from the golf course.
2. Then there's the "keep the family tree balanced" game. It goes something like this: You have twenty second cousins, but are close to only two of them. You want them to be at your wedding. But, family members and some etiquette books say you must invite all twenty, or none! The reason is to avoid hurt feelings in the rest of the family. In most cases, although the other eighteen second cousins could probably care less; their parents may get worked up about your leaving them off the list. The decision is up to you—but family feuds often start with this type of situation.
3. A decision not to invite children can also be an emotional minefield. Children in the wedding party are obviously included, as are brothers and sisters of the bride and groom. For the rest, if you want one child there, all children should be invited. The proper way to invite children is to include their names on the inside invitation envelope. According to etiquette, if their names aren't on this envelope, they're not invited. Another way to emphasize the fact that you don't want children in attendance is to put "Reception for Adults" on your reception card. You see, many parents either don't know proper etiquette about envelope addressing, or choose to ignore it. Out of towners may have difficulty attending if they can't find a sitter. Help them locate one if at all possible. Remember, if you break down when some parent pleads with you to make an exception, all the other parents who left their children at home might be angry with you. If excluding children becomes too much of a battle, hire a reliable sitter to watch them for the evening. Make sure it's someone who won't go off and join in the celebration.

The bride's family usually addresses and mails the invitations and announcements. If either of you have friends or family that live out of town, you might want to call or drop a note with the details in advance so they can make plans and necessary travel arrangements. It is very helpful to provide them with hotel information and a map of your area. If a large number are coming in, you may be able to negotiate a discount rate for them if they all stay in the same location. However, you aren't responsible for making the reservations or paying for the room.

- Guests should come to the ceremony site about fifteen minutes before the scheduled beginning.
- They stand when the wedding march begins, and follow the customs of the service they are attending.
- Wait to leave their seats until after the wedding party and honored guests have been escorted out.
- If you have a receiving line after the ceremony, they should pass through it and offer congratulations.
- Any guest who is invited to the reception is expected to let the couple know if they're coming. If a response card wasn't included with the invitation, they should do this with a handwritten note before your wedding day.
- At the reception, they should go through the receiving line (even if they went through one after the ceremony) and respond to any toasts made.
- They should wear proper clothing to the ceremony and reception. Traditionally, women wear knee-length dresses to daytime weddings, and long dresses in the evening. Men match their attire to the women they're escorting, and generally wear suits unless other styles are specified on the invitation.
- They should wait for you and your groom to finish your first dance before joining in.
- Give a wedding gift appropriate to their means.
- Thank the hosts of the affair (usually your parents) before leaving.

Photographer/Video

This is going to be a highly emotional day for you, and you'll be busy, hectic, and distracted a great deal of the time. You'll miss some things, and forget others. Let photographs capture the images of this special experience to enhance your memories. If you can possibly afford it, hire a professional. He can take pictures that won't include distracting backgrounds, but will show everyone at their best. It takes talent to capture the expressions, feelings, and emotions of a wedding. Choose the person who will record these memories with care.

**PROFESSIONAL
PHOTOGRAPHER**

An experienced photographer knows how to film different religious ceremonies, and to use lighting and equipment in the best way. He has the skills to foresee and capture events while they're happening. Best of all, he won't be distracted by joining in the celebration. A good photographer should provide clear, sharp pictures. The best can make a posed shot look like a candid one.

Most offer a variety of package deals. They usually include a combination of candid shots, formal poses, and optional special effects photos. Although they'll take hundreds of pictures on your wedding day, your final album will contain a set number of 8 × 10's, 5 × 7's, 4 × 5's, and so on.

**CHOOSING YOUR
PHOTOGRAPHER**

His style should match your personalities. A highly recommended expert may not take the type of pictures you prefer. You should also like him personally. You'll be spending a good part of a very important day with him; animosity between the two of you would provide upsetting distractions. Many busy professionals are booked well in advance, so if you know of a good photographer, ask him early to reserve your date.

The best way to find a photographer is to visit the studio and look through pictures he's already taken. He'll have albums that contain a composite of the weddings he's done. Remember he'll only put his best work in those books. Here are some points to consider as you examine them:

- Do all the pictures look alike?
- Are they only of traditional poses?
- Has he caught people at awkward moments?
- Are there photographs taken at bad angles?
- Does the background detract from the picture?
- Does he seem to have a good sense of timing?
- Does he seem to capture the emotions and expressions of the day?
- Do you have the general impression that the photographer is creative?

Larger studios use several photographers. If you find an album you especially like, ask for the name of the photographer. Is he available on your wedding date? Can you specify that he will be the one to take the pictures? If he isn't there, make an appointment to meet and talk about your wedding. As I mentioned before, you want to be sure you get along personally before you hire him. Here are some points you'll want to cover:

- How long has he been in the business?
- Does he do many weddings?
- What kind of packages are available?
- What is their cost?
- How much deposit is required?
- Until what date can it be refunded?
- How soon will the proofs be ready after the wedding?
- The final pictures?
- Who selects the final pictures—you or the photographer?
- Does the quoted cost include the finished album?
- Can you choose the album style?
- What is the cost of extra prints?
- How long does he keep the negatives? If you lose your photographs in a fire ten years from now, could they be replaced?

The Professional Photographers of America has a code of ethics, so ask if he's a member. You'll also want to check with the Better Business Bureau and make sure no complaints have been registered against him or the company. If you compare several photographers, be sure you compare the same things between each.

When you make your decision, be sure that your contract spells out the arrangements in detail, including:

- The number of photographers assigned to you
- Each place they're expected to take photographs.
- What time they'll arrive and depart.
- If you'll be charged overtime and at what rate.

VIDEO TAPING

Many photography studios offer this option, or you can obtain some names through recommendations and the yellow pages. This is a great way to capture the moments of your wedding day in a lively, realistic fashion. Most have sample videos for you to view. Ask to see them on as large a screen as possible (you can miss a lot on those little monitors). Again, don't forget that you'll be seeing their best work. Many criteria that apply to still photographs can be set against a video tape. Watch for:

- Clarity
- Color
- Camera movements
- Editing
- Has he caught people at awkward moments?
- Is the film shot at bad angles?
- Does the background detract from the picture?
- Does he seem to have a good sense of timing?
- Do his photos depict good taste?
- Do you have the general impression that he is creative?

Once again, meet with the photographer and make sure you get along. Find out details such as:

- How long has he been in business?
- Does he do many weddings?
- What kind of packages are available?
- What is their cost?
- How much deposit is required?
- Until what date can it be refunded?
- Who is responsible for damaged equipment?
- Will they keep a copy of the master tape?
- For how long?
- How much will it cost for extra copies of the tape?
- How many cameras will be used?
- Do they have equipment that works well in low light situations?
- Who will do the editing? Does this person have references?
- Will they attend the rehearsal? (Gives them a better idea of camera positioning if they know where your attendants, singers, readers, etc. will be. They should position unobtrusively so they don't block the view of members of the congregation, or distract from the ceremony.)

Most offer an option that allows you to wear microphones during the ceremony to have your vows on tape. (If it's a church wedding make sure this is acceptable to the minister).

You can have a more elaborate video, perhaps a combination of: still photos that include your baby and childhood pictures, the two of you together at your favorite places, personal messages to each other, close friends and family talking about you to the camera, photos from the pre-wedding parties, and anything else you'd like to include.

A tape of the ceremony only, where just one camera is used, could run as little as $180. A two camera package that includes all the major events might be $700. Complete coverage of the whole day will probably involve several photographers and lots of editing, and could cost thousands. Check them out, just as you would other services, and be sure your contract covers all the details. Before you sign, make sure that your ceremony and reception site can accommodate video cameras. Some can't and it's better to ask than to waste money.

A wedding video is a wonderful, lively momento of your wedding day, and can capture much more than still photographs. It's great if you can afford it.

NON-PROFESSIONAL PHOTOGRAPHER

It may seem easier and less expensive to ask a friend to take the wedding pictures. The results will depend on what type of photographs you're willing to accept, and how talented your friend is. If you just can't afford a professional, it might work better if you ask several different people to take pictures at your wedding, each for a certain time period. This way no one will miss all the fun. After all, they're supposed to be guests and it's not fair to ask them to work all night.

You might come up with many quality shots through sheer numbers. You still have to pay to have them developed, and wade through them to find the best photographs. The most common complaints among couples who had amateurs photograph their wedding were:

- Important pictures missed.
- No traditional, formal photographs.
- Lost several roles of exposed film.
- Most of the pictures came out badly.
- Spent too much time partying and hardly took any pictures.

Talk about these potential problems with your photographers before the wedding day. Whoever you choose, make sure they have access to proper equipment. If necessary, it can be rented. Naturally, you only want people you can trust to do the job.

STYLE OF ALBUM

Meet with your photographer several weeks in advance to finalize the arrangements. Discuss the type of pictures you want taken, the sequence of events, and family members that shouldn't be missed. Do you want many candid shots or prefer to rely on the traditional, formal pictures? Candid shots are better for capturing the mood of the day, but there's less control over how the picture will turn out. He must take a lot more photographs to get good candids, and you might not like having your picture taken so often. Most couples choose a wedding package that's a combination of candid and formal poses.

PHOTOGRAPHER'S CHECKLIST

Here's a list of the traditional wedding photographs. Study the ideas carefully, and place a check by the ones that appeal to you. There is also a space to add special ideas. You'll want to go over the plans for the day with your photographer, and discuss this checklist and other details. For example: How should he respond to guests who ask him to take specific pictures?

WEDDING DAY PHOTOGRAPHS

Before the Ceremony

Arrival Time: _____ Location:_____

Bride

☐ Alone close-up	☐ Alone—full length
☐ With mother	☐ With father
☐ With both parents	☐ With sisters
☐ With brothers	☐ With whole family
☐ With bridesmaids	☐ With maid of honor
☐ At gift table	☐ Adjusting veil
☐ Adjusting garter	☐ Touching up makeup
☐ With flowers	☐ Leaving with father
☐ Special/Other _____	

At the Ceremony Site

Arrival Time: _____ Location: _____

Bride
- ☐ Arriving
- ☐ In dressing room
- ☐ Special/Other _____
- ☐ Alone in processional
- ☐ Escorted in processional

Groom
- ☐ Arriving
- ☐ With best man
- ☐ Special/Other _____
- ☐ Before ceremony
- ☐ With his parents

Family
- ☐ Bride's mother
- ☐ Bride's father
- ☐ Special/Other _____
- ☐ Groom's mother
- ☐ Groom's father

Guests
- ☐ Arriving
- ☐ Group outside church
- ☐ Special/Other _____
- ☐ Group inside church
- ☐ Being seated

Ushers/Groomsmen
- ☐ Receiving boutonnieres
- ☐ Group in processional
- ☐ Special/Other _____
- ☐ Escorting guests
- ☐ Alone in processional

Bridesmaids
- ☐ Receiving flowers
- ☐ Group in processional
- ☐ Special/Other _____
- ☐ Lining up
- ☐ Alone in processional

Children
- ☐ Ring Bearer
- ☐ Pages
- ☐ Special/Other _____
- ☐ Flower Girl

During the Ceremony

☐ Groom waiting
☐ Bride given away
☐ Standing at altar
☐ Exchanging vows
☐ Exchanging kiss
☐ Bride at Mary's shrine
☐ Soloist
☐ Special/Other _____

☐ Meeting at altar
☐ Couple under canopy/trellis
☐ Kneeling at altar
☐ Exchanging rings
☐ Lighting candles
☐ Groom at Joseph's shrine
☐ Organist

Recessional

☐ Couple leaving altar
☐ Bridal party group
☐ Parents leaving
☐ Couple in receiving line
☐ Guests in receiving line
☐ Arch of Swords
☐ Special/Other _____

☐ Couple coming down the aisle
☐ Bridal party individual
☐ Guests leaving
☐ Parents in receiving line
☐ Throwing rice
☐ Minister with couple

Formal

☐ Bride alone
☐ Groom alone
☐ Couple at altar
☐ Bride with family
☐ At stained glass window
☐ Special/Other _____

☐ Bride with attendants
☐ Groom with attendants
☐ Group at altar
☐ Groom with family
☐ Both families together

Between Wedding and Reception

Time Available: _____   Locations:_____

☐ Cars being decorated
☐ Couple in back seat
☐ At park or other attractive site: _____
_____
_____
☐ Special/Other _____

☐ Couple in car
☐ Cars driving off

At the Reception Site
Arrival Time: _____   Location:_____

Bride and Groom
☐ Arriving   ☐ With attendants
☐ Hands with rings   ☐ With children
☐ In receiving line   ☐ During toasts
☐ During dinner   ☐ With friends
☐ Talking to guests   ☐ Cutting cake
☐ During first dance   ☐ In Grand March
☐ _____   ☐ _____

Groom
☐ With best man   ☐ With parents
☐ With grandparents   ☐ With friends
☐ With bride's parents   ☐ Tossing garter
☐ With godparents   ☐ Dancing
☐ Talking with guests   ☐ _____

Bride
☐ With maid of honor   ☐ With parents
☐ With grandparents   ☐ With friends
☐ With groom's parents   ☐ Tossing bouquet
☐ With godparents   ☐ Dancing
☐ Talking with guests   ☐ _____

Misc.
☐ Floral decorations   ☐ Musicians
☐ Cake table   ☐ Buffet table
☐ Honor table   ☐ Guest book
☐ Guests dancing   ☐ Grand March
☐ _____   ☐ _____
☐ _____   ☐ _____

INSTRUCTIONS FOR SPECIAL SITUATIONS

☐ Catch special guests such as: _____
☐ Take multi-generation picture of: _____
☐ Take group picture of (cousins, siblings, children,
  a certain generation) _____
☐ Special effects photos such as: _____
☐ Eliminate _____ photos if running out of time
  between the wedding and reception.
☐ Take or ☐ Do Not Take photographs suggested by guests.
  The only persons authorized to suggest photographs other
  than the bride and groom are _____
☐ _____ (person) will be on hand to point out people
  to photograph—identify grandparents, godparents

Step by Step Guide to Planning the Details

Ceremony

TYPE OF CEREMONY

It's easy to get caught up in the flurry of wedding plans, and forget the point of the day—your promise of commitment to one another. You may select a ceremony traditional to your religious faith, one adapted for inter-faith marriages, or a non-denominational service. Talk to your minister or wedding officiant about the ceremony they'll use. If you would like to make some changes—ask. Many mainline churches have specific items you can pick and choose among, others allow no adjustments to their ceremony. See sections on *Religious Ceremonies* and *Personalizing Your Ceremony* for further details.

Some couples (or churches) do not want flash photos taken during the ceremony. If that applies to your wedding, ask the officiant to announce just before it begins that photographs are prohibited during the ritual.

MARRIAGE LICENSE

Regulations vary throughout the States and from county to county. Check your city or county clerk's office for the requirements you must follow. Generally, you'll need to provide:

☐ Proof of age such as a birth certificate (if you're underage you'll need your parents to give their consent)
☐ If either of you have been divorced, bring the final decree.
☐ If applicable, bring proof of citizenship.
☐ Documentation of required blood and medical tests.
☐ Necessary fees.

The waiting period between the issuance of the license and the ceremony date will vary, as will the amount of time the certificate remains valid. Be sure you're familiar with the necessary regulations in advance to avoid problems.

CEREMONY SEATING

The groom designates one man as head usher, and he's responsible for coordinating the rest. (The best man is busy helping the groom). If there's a list of guests for a reserved section, or any special last minute instructions, the head usher will relay them to the others. Remember that most ushers may not be aware of all the fine details of seating. It's not a bad idea to photocopy this section and ask your fiance to pass it out to them a few days before the wedding.

They are to stand to the left of the inside door. As guests arrive, the usher asks if they are with the bride or groom, and seats them accordingly. In Christian religious denominations, your family is seated on the left, the groom's on the right. The opposite is true for Jewish weddings. Here are the customary traditions for the most common situations:

- [ ] If the guests do not have pew cards to present to the ushers for the reserved section, give the head usher a list of guests to be seated there. Ideally he'll be able to identify them to the others.
- [ ] Your parents, brothers, and sisters sit in the first pew on their respective sides. Grandparents, and other close relatives sit in the second pew. In longer ceremonies (such as a Nuptial Mass) the attendants sit in the first pew, the parents, siblings, etc. in the second, grandparents and others in the third.
- [ ] All other guests are seated from the front to back as they enter the church or ceremony site.
- [ ] The usher offers his arm to a female guest and unhurriedly escorts her to a seat on the proper side.
- [ ] A male guest is escorted to his seat, but the usher wouldn't offer his arm unless the guest was quite elderly and/or having difficulty walking.
- [ ] If a lady arrives with a male escort, the usher offers his arm to the lady, her escort follows behind.
- [ ] If two ladies arrive together, the usher should offer his arm to the eldest. The other can follow behind, or wait for another usher to escort her.
- [ ] Children under the age of fifteen usually follow their parents unescorted.
- [ ] As it nears time for the ceremony to begin, the ushers should seat guests to balance out the sides if one is noticeably more crowded than the other. A perfect balance isn't necessary, but twenty people on one side and one-hundred on the other is a terrible imbalance. The only 'rule' is that immediate family sit on opposite sides.
- [ ] It's acceptable to make quiet conversation while escorting the guest up the aisle.
- [ ] If yours is a military wedding, high-ranking officers should receive seats near the front.
- [ ] Five minutes before the mother of the bride is seated, the groom's mother is seated by the head usher. The groom's father would follow behind. They're seated in aisle seats of the first pew on the groom's side. However, in many ceremonies today all of the parents join the processional and seat themselves in their traditional places.
- [ ] If she doesn't take part in the processional, the bride's mother is escorted to her seat by the head usher, and her entrance is the signal that the processional is ready to begin.
- [ ] No one else is formally seated after the bride's mother. The aisle carpet is laid and the church doors closed. (Late arriving guests are allowed in, but asked to stand in the vestibule until the processional is completed. They would then seat themselves in the back).
- [ ] In some areas, it's customary for ushers to escort honored guests out of the building after they've participated in the recessional.
- [ ] Ushers 'bow out' each row of remaining guests (beginning in the front) after the recessional. This allows an orderly dismissal after the ceremony, and for your closest friends and relatives to congratulate you first.

SEATING FOR DIVORCED PARENTS

If either of your parents are divorced, seating arrangements can go haywire. Here are a few suggestions to make your job easier:

☐ If neither parent has remarried and are on amiable terms, it is acceptable for them to sit side by side in the first row.

☐ If both have remarried: Some believe that the mother always gets the first pew, no matter what. Others that it should go to the parent that raised you. Whichever you choose, they would be seated with their current spouse. The other parent and spouse would be seated in the second pew, on the aisle.

☐ Parents should always be seated on the aisle. If one is remarried and the other isn't, or if they had joint custody, it can get more complicated, especially if they're not on good terms. Ask your officiant for suggestions. You should definitely instruct your ushers about the seating arrangements you've worked out for this situation.

PROCESSIONAL/ RECESSIONAL

The order the wedding party walks up the aisle before the ceremony (processional) and down the aisle afterward (recessional) are worked out at the wedding rehearsal. To give you a general idea, I've included the lineup for traditional processionals in Christian and Jewish weddings. There are many variations to these, and your officiant may have other suggestions. The recessional is almost always the reverse of the processional, except that the groom escorts the bride. Traditionally, the bride is escorted up the aisle by her father. If your father is deceased, or unable to attend, you can be accompanied by your step-father, brother, friend, or any male relative. In many weddings today, your mother, or even both sets of parents join the bride in the processional.

CHRISTIAN	JEWISH
Ushers	Ushers
Bridesmaids	Bridesmaids
Maid of Honor	Rabbi
Ringbearer	Best Man
Flower Girl	Groom between his parents
Bride with escort	Maid of Honor
	Flower Girl and Ringbearer
	Bride between her parents

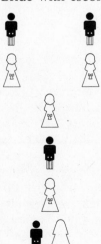

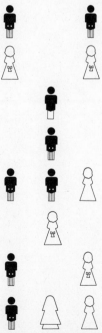

115

BETWEEN CEREMONY AND RECEPTION

Depending on the amount of time between the two, you can go somewhere especially pretty for photographs, drive around a bit, return to your mother's house to rest and relax, or have a small intimate party.

If the time gap is large, you might want to arrange an activity—especially if there are many out of town guests. Sometimes the groom's parents or another relative offer to host such a gathering. Some reception sites arrange a hospitality suite with cocktails and hors d'oeuvres for a small party. You and the groom don't have to attend.

Reception Details

Your party will have it's own format and atmosphere. In case you need some guidelines, I've outlined the basic, formal reception along with some common customs.

RECEIVING LINE

This is where the reception begins, so that you can greet your guests and make them feel welcome. Traditionally, it's formed just inside the entrance of the reception site, generally in the following order from the door:

> Bride's mother (or hostess of the reception)
> Groom's father (optional)
> Groom's mother (or step-mother, guardian, etc.)
> Bride's father (optional)
> Bride
> Groom
> Maid/Matron of Honor
> Best Man
> Bridesmaids (optional)
> Groomsmen (optional)

Children in the wedding party such as flower girls and ringbearer do not stand in the receiving line.

It's a good idea to examine the guest list before the wedding, and to practice pronouncing the more difficult names in the groom's family. Don't panic, no one will expect you to remember everyone's name, or say it perfectly. As someone with a difficult to pronounce name, believe me, I take errors for granted.

Try to greet each guest. Introduce your groom to guests he doesn't know, and he will do the same for you. If you don't know who the person is, smile and ask. Guests express their best wishes to the bride and congratulate the groom. There'll be much kissing and handshaking. Say a few polite words to each, but save lengthy discussions for later. You don't want to hold up the line.

If your palms sweat easily, rub a small amount of cream anti-perspirant on them. Don't allow anyone to smoke in the receiving line. It's a fire hazard, and can be irritating to guests.

When all the guests have arrived (or when there are none in sight and it's getting late) the line can disperse. Give everyone a few minutes to regain their composure and freshen up.

DINNER SEATING

If dinner will be served, the wedding party take their places at the head table to signal that the toasts and the meal are about to begin. At most receptions everyone at the head table is seated facing the crowd, as follows:

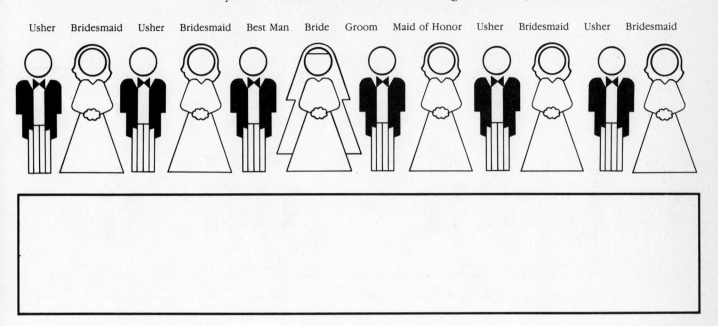

Usher Bridesmaid Usher Bridesmaid Best Man Bride Groom Maid of Honor Usher Bridesmaid Usher Bridesmaid

If you prefer rectangular seating, here's a possible arrangement:

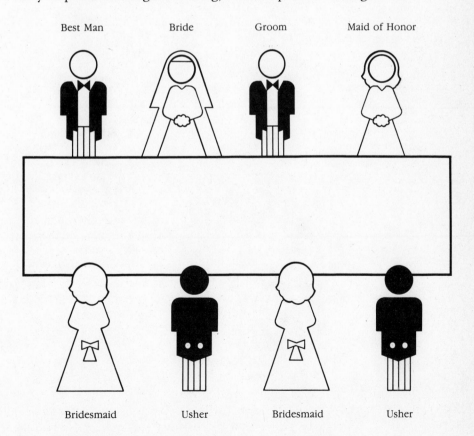

Best Man   Bride   Groom   Maid of Honor

Bridesmaid   Usher   Bridesmaid   Usher

Children in the wedding party do not have to be seated at the head table. Generally, the seating includes you and your groom at the center, with best man and maid of honor flanking you. Bridesmaids, groomsmen, and ushers would also be seated there. Parents of the bride and groom can be seated at the head table, or if you have a large wedding party you might have a separate honors table that would include parents, clergy, grandparents, siblings, godparents, children in the wedding party, and any special guests. Divorced parents of the new couple should not be seated together. It's best for them to host individual tables. The seating at an honor table will depend on the size of your tables, as well as the number of people to be seated at them. Here is a possible seating arrangement for an honor table:

1. Bride's mother
2. Groom's father
3. Officiant's wife
4. Bride's father
5. Officiant
6. Groom's sister
7. Groom's mother
8. Bride's brother
9. Grandfather
10. Godmother/Aunt
11. Godfather/Uncle
12. Grandmother

Have place cards at the head table and honor tables to avoid confusion and embarrassment. Prepare them (and a seating chart) in advance, and have your caterer (or maid of honor) put them out before the reception. Most brides do not prepare seating charts for all the guests at a large wedding reception.

If you decide to arrange all the seating, remember to put each person near someone they know, yet give everyone an opportunity to meet new people. Alternate men and women every other chair, and according to etiquette you shouldn't seat a husband and wife next to each other. Remember to separate people who don't like each other. Number the tables, and have the caterer put place cards at each setting. Place a large seating chart near the guest book listing each person's name and their table number so that each person can find his seat.

Rounded tables allow for the best of friendly interchanges, but shouldn't seat more than ten each. Don't seat elderly guests too close to the musicians.

TOASTING

After the receiving line has dispersed, and you are seated for the meal, the toasting beverage is served. The best man begins by standing up and introducing himself and the wedding party (it wouldn't hurt to have the names written out for him beforehand). He then proposes his first toast to you and your groom. The groom will make the next toast, saluting you. When you're being toasted you should remain seated and not sip from your glass. Sip between toasts. When someone toasts you, smile and nod your head in their direction.

DRINKING

Because weddings are a celebration, the party can get out of hand if alcohol is served and guests have imbibed too freely. You know your friends and family well enough to know if this is a possibility. Have a talk with your most uninhibited guests beforehand, and ask them to keep things under control. Not only would smashed glasses, dancing on tables, and swinging from chandeliers take away from the dignity of your party—damages can be expensive. Instruct your security to end any arguments as soon as they begin—such incidents can serve as catalysts for more trouble.

You don't want a tragedy after your wedding. Taxi and limousine services are available for drivers who have celebrated more than they should. Find the names, numbers and costs for several, and have the bandleader announce their availability to the crowd. Someone (perhaps the bartenders) should have the telephone numbers handy. It's also an idea to post a note next to the pay phone. Encourage your guests to call and make use of those services.

DINNER

Don't let the toasting continue too long. Have the best man rise and announce when it's time for dinner to be served. If a blessing will be offered before the meal, he should instruct guests to stand or stay seated, then introduce the person who will say grace. If your clergyman is present, he would do the honors. Otherwise, ask a special friend or relative ahead of time. The head table and honor table are served dinner first.

After the meal, it's time for you and your groom to rise and circulate among your guests. Try to say a few words to everyone, and be sure to thank them for coming. Offer a special thank you to those who contributed to the day, financially or otherwise.

CUTTING THE CAKE

Your wedding cake should be placed in an area that everyone can view, but out of the main line of traffic. Don't place it too close to the receiving line, or anywhere it could be easily overturned. At a dinner reception, the cake should be cut about thirty minutes after the meal. If you aren't having a dinner, it's customary to do it about one hour after the receiving line ends. If you prefer a different time, that's fine. Just let the photographer and caterer know what time that will be. The cake is usually cut with a knife that's decorated with ribbons and flowers, often purchased especially for the occasion. Place your hand on the knife, and your new husband places his hand over yours. You cut the first slice together, then you feed a part of the slice to him. He feeds the rest to you—symbolic of the sharing you'll be doing for the rest of your lives.

DANCING

It begins with a slow dance with just you and your groom, usually to a romantic song with special meaning to both of you. If the band has been playing background music, at the appointed time they should announce that the bride and groom will now begin the dancing. After a few minutes, it is customary for your father to cut in, while the groom dances with your mother. After that, there's a traditional order of dancing among the wedding party that goes like this:

- Groom's father would dance with the bride, and groom with his mother.
- Bride and the best man, groom and the maid of honor.
- Groom dances with all the female attendants, the bride will all the males.

About the time you're dancing with the best man, the floor should start filling with guests. If not, encourage your attendants to keep dancing until it does. Make sure you get plenty of dances with your new husband before the evening's over.

GARTER-BOUQUET TOSS

About 1/2 hour before you leave, or before the Grand March, have the bandleader or the best man get everyone's attention. First, unmarried males are asked to gather round. You are seated, with the groom standing next to you. With fanfare from the band, he removes your garter and tosses it over his shoulder to the waiting crowd. Then the unmarried females gather around you, as you toss your bouquet over your shoulder to them. The person who catches the garter or bouquet is considered lucky, and the next to marry.

GRAND MARCH

This is a traditional custom among some ethnic backgrounds. At a pre-arranged time well into the reception (usually around 10:00 pm), the band leader will announce that it's time for the Grand March to begin. You and your groom lock arms, and followed by your attendants and guests, lead the crowd about the room while the band plays lively music. You make a number of passes around the room, and some grooms have led the crowd outside and around the building. It's a fun-filled time with much laughter and merriment. At the end, you form a new receiving line with your wedding party next to a long table.

As guests wait to greet you, they can help themselves to pieces of cake; as well as cigars and shots of whiskey (traditionally supplied by your father). Many will take one glass for themselves and one for the groom (or you). When they reach you, they hand you the glass so you can drink together. This receiving line is your last chance to visit with them because you'll be leaving soon.

120

When the last person has passed through the line, the bandleader asks the guests to form a circle with you and your new husband in the center. First you are seated and the maid of honor (or your mother) removes your veil. The band begins to play *Let Me Call You Sweetheart* and you and the groom waltz around the inside of the circle. The guests and wedding party hold hands and slowly circle round you, singing with the band. At the end of the song, the two of you swiftly break away and leave the party.

Tell your security to keep a special eye on the gifts during the Grand March; this is their most vulnerable time.

LEAVE TAKING   If you won't have a Grand March, at some point after the garter and bouquet are tossed, you both say a private goodbye to your parents and slip away. If you'd like your guests to stay and enjoy themselves, have the bandleader or the your father announce that they are welcome to stay. Otherwise, the reception tends to end after you and your new husband leave.

Food/Catering

It's customary to have a celebration that includes cake and champagne or punch after the wedding ceremony. Any additional food and beverages would depend on the time of day and size of your reception. There are wedding breakfasts, luncheons, or dinners. Others feature snacks, light sandwich buffets, or hors d'oeuvres. A lot will depend on local and ethnic traditions, or those of common sense. Don't have a reception at dinnertime without a dinner. The larger the guest list, the greater variety of food you should provide.

The meal is the biggest part of the wedding budget, but there are many ways of obtaining food. If it's a small, informal affair you might prepare it yourselves, or ask each guest to bring a dish. Catered dinners are always used at larger, more formal weddings. Caterers offer a selection of foods to pick from, and you choose the menu. Because the dinner is so expensive, and is such a big part of the reception, it's important to be very careful when choosing a caterer.

There are different types of caterers too. Some come with the reception site—especially if it's a hotel ballroom or restaurant. Others contract out every detail, supplying the dinnerware, meal, decorations, cake, bartenders, and beverages. You can pick and choose the services you want them to provide, and contract for the rest elsewhere. Then there are those that only prepare and serve the food.

Most charge a flat fee based on the amount of food they provide. It's usually divided as place servings, so if you tell them 200 guests will be at the reception, you'll be charged for 200 place servings. That's why it's so important for guests to return their response cards. If only 170 people are coming, you can save the cost of thirty place servings. Ask if tips are included in the costs, if not (and the service was satisfactory) add 15% to the total on the bill when you pay it.

You want a caterer that you feel comfortable communicating with. As with all service providers, the best are booked first. Ask around, word of mouth is often the best source for a good caterer. Be sure to ask if anything went wrong, and what the caterer's strong points are. (If it's gourmet food and that's not in your plan, you won't be interested). You definitely want to interview your caterer personally. Be sure to have all the facts prepared—the date, time, place of reception, number of guests, and a general idea of what you want (keep costs down, elaborate production, etc.). Here's a worksheet that covers important items you'll want to learn from each caterer when you interview them.

CATERING WORKSHEET		
Name #1: Phone		
Name #2: Phone		
QUESTION	#1	#2
How long in business?		
Do you have photos of wedding meals you have catered?		
Can you provide me with references?		
What services do you provide?		
How do you determine your fee?		
Are taxes and tips included?		
What is your typical menu?		
Can you provide special meals (kosher, diabetic, etc.)?		
Are coffee, tea, cream, sugar included with the meal?		

QUESTION	#1	#2
If not, what's the charge?		
Are tablecloths, napkins, dinnerware, flatware, glassware, included? Charge?		
What's the estimated cost per plate?		
Is this for a dinner served family style (seated) or buffet style?		
How much staff will serve my wedding?		
Do you decorate the tables?		
What type of decorations do you supply?		
Do you set out place cards?		
Do you cut the cake? Extra charge?		

QUESTION	#1	#2
What happens with leftover food?		
If we get it, are containers provided?		
Do you supply bartenders? Cost?		
Order liquor? Costs involved?		
What about overtime?		
What deposit amount is required?		
When is balance due?		
Until what date can it be refunded?		
When is the final guest count due?		
Can I change it? Extra charge for that?		

FOOD QUANTITIES

If you are not using a caterer, perhaps one of the most difficult determinations to make is how much food to buy and prepare. The following chart provides information about the amount of food needed for a group of either 36 or 100 people. If you are planning a party for 72, multiply the amounts for thirty-six servings by two. If you are planning fifty, cut the amounts for one-hundred in half.

You should not serve every item listed, but pick and choose among them. For example: A menu of ham, potatoes, and canned vegetables for thirty-six people would require 13 pounds of ham, 13 pounds of potatoes, and 10 pounds of vegetables. (Don't forget to buy more canned vegetables because of water weight).

If you added chicken, rice, and a tossed salad to the menu you would reduce the quantities of every item on the menu. The greater variety of food you have, the less each individual item will be needed. There's no perfect formula for estimating how much you should reduce each item. If you want each person to have all the ham and chicken they want, and don't mind leftovers, you would serve a great deal more than if you expected to provide a modest selection.

Using the same example, you might also try to determine how many will eat ham, and how many chicken. The best rule of thumb for meat is to determine the amount needed for the number of people you are serving and add 20%. For example, if you purchase ham and beef for 36 people, you could purchase sixteen pounds. The three extra pounds create a margin of safety. If you are serving three meats, use the same formula, but add 30%

FOOD QUANTITY CHART

ITEM	36 People	100 People
Meat		
Ham	13 lbs.	38 lbs.
Beef, Veal, Pork	13 lbs.	38 lbs.
Chicken (no other meat)	2 1/2 pieces per person	
Chicken (with other meat)	1 1/2 pieces per person	
Side Dishes		
Potatoes	13 lbs.	38 lbs.
Rice	4 lbs.	11 lbs.
Vegetables	10 lbs.	28 lbs.
Head Lettuce	5 medium	14 medium
Extras		
Butter squares	3/4 pound	2 lbs.
Bread (with meal)	1 1/2 slices per person	
Bread (for sandwich)	3 to 4 slices per person	
Ice Cream	2 gallons	6 gallons
Beverages		
Soda Pop	8 quarts	24 quarts
Coffee	1 1/2 lbs.	4 lbs.
Tea	1/4 lb.	1/2 lb.
Cream	1 1/2 quarts	4 quarts
Sugar	1 pound	2 1/2 lbs.

Wedding Cake

One of the strongest traditions (after rings and flowers), is the wedding cake. It's shape, flavor, and decorations are a matter of personal taste—and there's a huge variety of options to choose from. The size will depend on the number of guests you will be serving.

Some individuals do a healthy business making cakes in their homes. Or your caterer or local bakery might provide the one you prefer. When making your decision, you must determine the following:

☐ Are they reliable? (Will they have it completed on time)?
☐ Can they cook? (Will it taste good)?
☐ Are they talented decorators? (Will it look good)?
☐ What do they charge? (Does it fit your budget)?

Most cakes aren't that expensive, unless you want a huge, elaborately decorated one. Prices are determined by size and decorations. There might be an extra charge if you ask for a special flavor. Sometimes there are non-edible ornaments such as decorative pillars or swans to separate layers; or fountains built into the cake. You usually pay a deposit on these items, and it's refunded when you return them.

The cake is traditionally topped with a specialty piece, such as figures of crystal bells or the bride and groom. This is saved as a keepsake, and is sometimes used on anniversary cakes. It's also customary to freeze the top layer of the cake after the wedding. You defrost it and share it on your first wedding anniversary.

Beverages

Any reception should include liquid refreshment for your guests. Punch is a good budget stretcher, and if it's non-alcoholic it can be used by both adults and children. Here are three punch recipes. Make a batch before your wedding to be sure that it suits your taste.

CHAMPAGNE PUNCH

Mix four parts champagne to two parts ginger ale, to one part fruit juice or grenadine syrup.

STRAWBERRY CHAMPAGNE PUNCH
Makes about 4 quarts

1 cup sugar
2 cups water
1 cup plain brandy
Ice
1 cup fresh, halved strawberries
20 oz frozen strawberries packed in syrup
1 quart chilled cranberry juice cocktail
2 bottles chilled champagne

Heat sugar and water in a saucepan until clear. Cool. Stir in brandy and frozen strawberries. Chill. When ready to serve, pour in champagne and cranberry juice cocktail. Add ice and fresh strawberries. Stir well until chilled.

NON-ALCOHOLIC PUNCH
Makes about 5 1/2 quarts

Mix two 64 oz bottles of 50/50 soda pop with one large can of Hawaiian Punch. This will fill an average punch bowl.

It's hard to decide the amount to buy if you must purchase your own beverages. The manager of your reception site, or a liquor dealer may be able to offer suggestions. Ask if they'll refund unopened bottles (some States have laws against this). That way you can purchase more than you need to make sure you'll have enough. Ask for a volume discount. Or watch for sales and purchase slowly in the months before the wedding.

As a rule, allow 8 oz. of liquid refreshments for each guest for every hour the reception is expected to last. More beverages are consumed in warm weather, and during evening receptions. When alcohol is served, people drink more no matter what time of the day.

Champagne/Wine: One 26 oz. bottle would yield about 6 servings.

Beer: One keg yields 15 gallons, or about 520 eight oz glasses.

Hard Liquor: A one gallon bottle should yield about 32 drinks. Be sure to compute additional amounts if you serve shots during toasts, and after the Grand March.

Soda Pop/Mix   For mixed drinks allow three parts mix to one part liquor. Plan for three sodas per person per hour for those who won't drink alcohol. (Adults will drink less, but children make up for it). Plan two to three mixed drinks per adult for the first hour, one to two mixed drinks per adult each hour after that.

Don't forget to arrange to have plenty of ice available. For an evening reception with 150 people, allow about 75 lbs. If you will be serving punch, you can freeze some of the non-alcoholic ingredients in a mold to help avoid a watered down taste.

Check the area around your reception site to see what establishments will be open late on your wedding night. If a quick trip for ice, pop, or liquor becomes necessary, you'll want to know where to send someone.

What Kind of Liquor Should You Purchase?

A great deal depends on the drinking habits of your guests. For the average formal reception, you can expect drinks to be served heavily as people arrive and during toasts; with social drinking throughout the rest of the evening. If your group will be primarily teetotalers, your level of consumption will be smaller and more consistent.

You also need to determine how many of your guests will drink hard liquor, as opposed to those who will consume beer or wine. You probably have some idea of the drinking habits of friends and family members; your fiance and both sets of parents can provide additional clues. Unless you're having a very elaborate affair, you don't have to offer a huge variety of alcoholic beverages. Here are some ideas of what to include:

Champagne: Can cost from $4 to $150+ per bottle. Traditionally, one glass is served to every guest to sip during toasts. The price you pay for each bottle has more to do with your budget than with the formality or informality of your reception. If you don't know which kind to buy, your liquor dealer will suggest a choice to fit your pocketbook. If you dislike champagne, try a sparkling wine instead. Those from Italy are called *Spumante,* from Germany they are *Sekt,* and *Cava* is from Spain. Your choice should have a pleasant odor, attractive color, with bubbles that continually rise to the top of the glass. Taste is a personal matter, some are sweet, others dry (labeled Natural). The best quality is about $17 a bottle, unless you want a deluxe French champagne. Those prestigious blends (such as Dom Perignon) could run $50 a bottle and more. A decent quality can be purchased for around $10 a bottle, the average is $7 to $12. Anything under $7 is probably bulk processed.

Wine   Have several bottles of white and red wines available for those who prefer to consume this beverage. Again, if you don't know which kind to buy, ask your dealer for suggestions. The average consumption is 2/3 white wine, 1/3 red. It's less expensive to buy it by the jug. Be sure the wine is chilled before serving.

Beer   Buy a keg, the cost per serving is much lower. If you're afraid of having leftover, you can supplement it with canned or bottled beer. Since beer loses it's taste when warm, buy small bottles and cans. Many are left sitting as people talk and dance, and much of it goes to waste.

Hard Liquor   Most reception bars serve whiskey, vodka, scotch, bourbon, gin, and rum. If you need to watch your budget, purchase generic or house brands.

Soda Pop/Mix   Popular mixes for drinks are Seven Up, Club Soda, Coca Cola, Ginger Ale, Tonic and Soda Water, Tomato Juice, and Orange Juice. These beverages can also be used by children and teetotalers. Buy large bottles and look for sales to keep costs down.

RECEPTION BAR   Liquor laws vary among states and communities. Liquor licenses spell out how and what can be served at each location. Regulations can vary among establishments, depending on the type of license they hold. For example: some can only serve beer and wine. Others, can only serve during certain time periods each day.

Each business sets it's own policy. At one, you must use the house liquor, and are charged a set rate for every bottle opened. At others, you furnish the liquor, but it's served by their personnel, and you're charged a cork fee for each bottle opened. Some sites leave the acquisition and serving of liquor entirely to you.

If you must hire your own bartender, obtain references and call them. If you end up with bartenders that don't do their jobs (drinking, dancing, serving too strong drinks) it'll be a waste of your money. Your caterer or reception site might have a list of recommended bartenders they can provide you.

Discuss how you want it to operate. Will the bar shut down during dinner? Should the drinks be pre-mixed? At most dinner receptions, the bar is open for cocktails, closed during the meal, then reopened for the rest of the evening. Some couples decide to have a cash bar to keep costs down. Guests must pay for their own drinks. This is unpopular with guests, and I don't blame them.

Music and Musicians

Music is a powerful way to set the mood for the gathering, and accentuate special moments. The ceremony can be joyful, soothing, inspiring, or reverent. The reception might be festive, romantic, light-hearted, or demure. Musical selections should reflect your personal preferences, but your guests should enjoy themselves too.

CEREMONY

Many couples try to express their deeper feelings for one another and the occasion through the music at their ceremony. Heinrich Heine, a nineteenth century writer, said that "When words leave off, music begins."

Although some churches restrict or control what music can be played at the ceremony, they usually have a selection you may choose from. You don't have to be limited to a soloist or organist. Here are some ideas to consider:

☐ Harp   ☐ Flute
☐ Violin   ☐ Guitar
☐ Piano   ☐ Trumpet
☐ String Quartet   ☐ Choir

RECEPTION

Plan for background music during dinner, with a different tempo for the social part of the evening. If you don't have dancing, that will probably mean a pianist, violinist, or a small combo of mixed instruments.

If you will have dancing, remember to request a variety of songs so that guests of all ages can enjoy a turn on the floor. Most people react best to the music that was popular in their teen years. In addition, there are many nice songs that are impossible to dance to—make sure the music you select has the right beat. List the songs you want to have played and give it to the band leader. Discuss timing. When will dinner begin? What should they play to announce the cake cutting, your first dance, throwing the bouquet/garter, and other special events?

PRE-RECORDED MUSIC

Live musicians can be quite expensive. Today, a popular alternative is to have pre-recorded music at the reception. It might cost $300 to $800, depending on the variety of music, equipment, and disk jockey. Some couples prefer songs they choose and record before the reception. A friend changes tapes when necessary.

Others have a disk jockey play his selection of tunes (which also allows more flexibility for personal requests). The disk jockey will also act as Master of Ceremonies, in the same manner as the band leader.

CHOOSING THE MUSICIANS

Keep their experience in mind if you ask friends or relatives to perform at the ceremony. If they've never performed in public before, they might get cold feet at the last minute. And you'll find yourself dashing around trying to find backups on a moment's notice. If you are hiring a soloist and organist, be sure they rehearse before the wedding if they've never worked together before. Whatever musician you choose, know their vocal range and abilities—and keep them in mind when selecting the music they will perform.

You don't want to spend a lot of money on an elegant wedding, then destroy that tone by booking inferior musicians to cut costs. Whether you pick a disk jockey or a live band, the best source is word of mouth, or through caterers, wedding consultants, and other wedding service providers. Don't hesitate to look for alternatives in the yellow pages, or contact the musician's union in your area. They'll provide a list of bands, the size of the group, style of music, price, and phone numbers. You'll want to listen to any group before you hire them, so your source for finding them isn't as important as their compatibility to your needs. But don't choose a band or DJ based on hearing them play at one event. A good performer will play differently to different groups.

Many reception bands offer videos of their performances for you to view, as well as audio tapes of each musician playing in different styles. Price is based on the size of the group, travel time, length of reception, and the popularity of the band. It could run anywhere from $650 to $2000 + for a six piece dance band.

You'll want to see them in action, especially regarding the tone they set for the evening. As Master of Ceremonies, the band leader might be discreet and low key, or he might be vivacious and outgoing—pulling members of the crowd into the act. The important thing is that you both are comfortable with his style. You also want to discuss attire—do you want them in tuxedos, suits, or less formal clothing?

Some couples ask that an audio tape be made of the music on their wedding night for future memories. If you like this option, find out if there'll be an additional charge before you order it.

MUSICIAN CHECKLIST		
	First	Second
Available on your date?		
Name of bandleader:		
Phone number:		
Will he/she be present?		
Number of musicians:		
Hourly rate:		
Overtime rate:		
How will partial hours be billed?		
Number of breaks:		
Length of breaks:		
Instruments available:		
Style specialize in:		
Allow your choices:		
Light System:		
Deposit required:		
Balance Due:		
Cancellation policy?		

Once you find the right band or DJ you will want to have a contract that spells out all the details. Don't forget the date, time, and place! Most will require a 50% deposit when you reserve your date. On average, they'll take a break every 45 minutes, although you can pay extra to have them play straight through. If you want continuous music, some supply tapes to be played during their breaks. Or you can bring your own (you'll need equipment), or hire a pianist to play during breaks. Refreshments should be available to the musicians.

MUSICAL SELECTIONS

Go over song choices well before the wedding, some provide a checklist for you to pick your selections, or indicate what shouldn't be played even if guests request it. Others ask you for a list of preferences. Select songs that will appeal to a wide range of ages and musical tastes.

Theme weddings seldom work, especially when it comes to the reception. Many couples who asked their musicians to provide only music from the 60's, or Jazz only end up changing their minds before the day is over. Your music is for the guests enjoyment too, and a variety should be played so that each has an opportunity to recognize and enjoy tunes. We always enjoy music more when we've heard it several times before. That doesn't mean you shouldn't let your musicians know the style you want emphasized (country, classical, ethnic, waltzes, Jazz, rock from the 50's, 60's, 70's, 80's, or current popular tunes).

If your selections are different from standard wedding fare, you must allow time for the music to be ordered. Be sure you have the exact title, composer/arranger, and the voice range and type of accompaniment needed. Order enough copies of each piece because photocopying sheet music is illegal.

If you're spending the money to hire professionals, utilize their expertise. Don't dictate each song in a certain order. Give them your wishes, and trust their judgement. They need the flexibility to adapt to the crowd and mood of the evening.

Transportation

If you've asked people from out of town to stand up in the wedding, you are responsible for transporting them throughout the day. In addition, transportation for the entire wedding party to all wedding-related functions should be properly co-ordinated.

You need to determine how many people need to be transported, where they must be picked up, and taken to. If you can afford it, it's a nice touch to rent limousines for your entire wedding party (or at least for the car that will transport you and your new husband). Incidentally, although you aren't responsible for paying for transportation for out of town guests, it's thoughtful to make sure their arrangements are also completed.

If you decide to add flair to the day, limousine services are available in most cities, look in the yellow pages of your telephone book. Call around, compare prices and services. Here are a few things to consider:

☐ Do they own or rent their vehicles? (Can affect condition and control of availability).
☐ Do they refund if you (or they) cancel?
☐ What does the driver wear?
☐ Cost per hour.
☐ Minimum charge.

☐ Any additional charges.
☐ Tipping policy.
☐ Insurance coverage.
☐ Additional mileage charge.
☐ Overtime (and how computed).

Go and see their cars before you rent them. You'll be asked to place a deposit and provide exact pick-up times, addresses, and destinations.

If you can't afford limousines, it's traditional to have friends and relatives handle the transportation with their own automobiles. It's a common practice for each groomsman to transport his bridesmaid throughout the day. Make sure they allow enough time to pick up the bridesmaids and be at the ceremony site one-half hour before the beginning, because their main job is to seat the guests.

Your best man may act as your personal chauffeur and drive you about that day (the maid of honor would join him). Ask friends or other relatives to transport any additional persons who have no way of getting to the functions. That might include out of towners and elderly guests who are unable to drive. Offer to pay for gas and a car wash—and be sure to have a few backup drivers in case there are problems.

Don't forget to tell each driver who they'll pick up, where, and when. And provide the passengers with the names of their 'chauffeur'. Give each the other's telephone number in case of emergencies. Have maps at the rehearsal dinner to make sure everyone knows how to get to the appointed sites.

If you want to add a personal touch, and it fits with the style and location of your wedding, you could try something unique. Here are a few rental ideas:

☐ Antique Car
☐ Horse-drawn Carriage
☐ Hot Air Balloon
☐ Fire Engine
☐ Horse-drawn Sleigh

Driver's Note Sheets	
Driver:	Phone #:
Pick Up:	Time:
Address:	Phone #:
Directions:	
Deliver to:	

Security

Uninvited guests can disrupt your party, steal from you and your guests, or destroy property. Disagreements can erupt among the guests. Minors may consume alcohol. Some people might bring drugs. You want someone to watch over the party, maintain order, and prevent disasters, mishaps, and illegal actions. Many halls, restaurants, or other reception locations provide their own security. Depending on the size of your crowd, the type of people, the neighborhood, and how accessible the location is to the general public, you may want to add some of your own. Naturally, if your reception site has no security, you'll want to hire several guards for better protection.

Your best bet is to hire off-duty police officers if it's permissible for them to moonlight in your area. (Some departmental regulations forbid this practice). Ask family or friends for recommendations, or call the department in the town where your reception site is located. You may also try nearby towns, county, and state police agencies. Ask the going rate to get an idea of what to offer. The most common practice is for you to place a notice on their bulletin board, and any interested officers will telephone you. Your notice should include:

Number of men needed:
Hourly rate of pay offered:
Times:
Date:
Location:
Your Name:
Your Phone #:

When an officer telephones, discuss the duties you expect of him, and any potential problems you anticipate. Don't forget to ask if he's willing to work overtime if necessary, and what he charges. Discuss how he usually handles uninvited guests, altercations, and overly indulgent revelers. In some states, the police officer will be liable if liquor is served to minors at your reception. If you think some members of your family might slip a few drinks to teenagers, discuss this with the officer now. He can suggest a tactful way to inform adults that this practice will be unacceptable.

If you prefer to hire a private security agency, check for listings in your phone book. Visit their office. Discuss their rates, and policies for handling uninvited guests, altercations, and overly indulgent revelers. The amount of authority vested in private agencies varies greatly. Find out what power and authority they have. Are they armed? Can they legally detain anyone? Do they have any special regulations? (Some will not work at receptions where liquor is served).

When you find an agency you like, be sure to have a written contract for their services. Most charge a minimum rate of working time—such as four hours. Make sure the computation for any additional charges such as overtime are clearly spelled out. If you want the guards dressed in a certain manner (uniforms, tuxedos, etc) be sure that you and the agency are in agreement beforehand.

The Big Day At Last

Rehearsal

You won't be the only one who's nervous before the wedding. Everyone from your mother to the flower girl will feel a few butterflies about their role. A rehearsal gives each person an opportunity to practice, and ease the worries that accompany the big day. It's usually held at the ceremony site, on the afternoon or evening before the wedding. Try to schedule it as early as possible, to allow time for a dinner afterwards. You want to be sure everyone will be well rested for the wedding.

All members of the wedding party should attend the rehearsal. If possible, the musicians, singers, and video photographers should also be there so that everyone can practice realistically. The officiant is experienced at running these, and will point out seating, take everyone through the processional and recessional, and tell you what to expect during the ceremony. He will usually establish signals or clues for persons to watch for so they know when to act. (Such as when the best man should produce the ring).

It might take several repetitions before everyone understands what's expected of them. Try to go easy on any children present, too much practicing might only tire and confuse them.

REHEARSAL DINNER

Traditionally, the groom's parents host this dinner after the rehearsal. It's a good idea to ask the officiant the approximate length of the rehearsal so that reservations can be made. Remember, it might run longer than expected, and you must allow travel time to the site. The gathering is usually held at a local restaurant, and includes all members of the wedding party, their spouses/fiance(e)s, and any special guests that would be appropriate.

Delay or Cancellation

After you have begun making your wedding plans, it's possible that something might occur that will make it necessary to delay your date. It might be illness, loss of job, or the desire to have more time before you take the big step. Whatever the case, if the invitations haven't been mailed, you only need to notify immediate family members, your closest friends, and members of your wedding party. If the invitations were mailed, you can contact guests by telephone, personal note, telegram, or in a large wedding a pre-printed card. Do not send the information by mail if the guests will not receive it at least one week before the wedding date. The following format can be used in written notification:

Mr. and Mrs. Robert Johnson announce
that the marriage of their daughter
Katherine Ann
to
Mr. William M. Thomas
will be postponed until _____.

Contact each place where you reserved your wedding date, even if you hadn't placed a deposit. If possible, change your reservation to the new date. If that isn't possible and you had placed a deposit, request a refund. You may not receive one, but it doesn't hurt to ask.

No one ever expects their wedding to be cancelled, but it can and does happen. You never have to give the reason to anyone but your closest family members and friends. Once again, if invitations have not been mailed, notify closest friends, family, and members of the wedding party. If they had been sent, and written notification would reach the guest within one week before your date, you can send a personal note or printed card, depending on the size of your guest list. If it's too late, everyone should be telephoned or telegrammed. Your note card might read as follows:

Mr. and Mrs. Robert Johnson announce
that the marriage of their daughter
Katherine Ann
to
Mr. William M. Thomas
will not take place.

Everyone who has reserved a date to provide services for you should be notified. Ask for any deposits to be refunded. Read your contract, in many cases you will not receive your refund. In some circumstances you may even be liable for the full amount if they can't find anyone for your date. They won't look very hard since they'll be paid in any case. Check with your State Attorney General's office for more details about your legal rights in such situations.

Return any gifts you received, including your engagement ring. If your attendants will lose their deposits on their gowns, reimburse them for the money they have spent.

Your Wedding Day

This is the day you've been working for, planning for, dreaming about. You're taking a big step, making a huge commitment. You're sharing it with the man you love, and your friends and family. You're celebrating the promise of your future.

It's normal to be nervous. Things go wrong at weddings. Most problems are minor, and even those who had major catastrophes survived them. And no matter how hard you try, there are going to be ruffled feathers, some of them yours, before the day is over.

Because there are so many details involved in planning a wedding, it's easy for problems to get blown out of proportion. You spend hours studying floral arrangements, only to hear at the last minute that your selection won't be possible because the flowers didn't arrive. You want everything to be perfect, so you panic. Try to keep it all in perspective. This is only one day, a small portion of your life. Mishaps will not doom your marriage. Some of the happiest couples we know had huge disasters at their weddings.

Try to remember that people will be there because they care about you. Most will also be wrapped up in themselves and won't be critiquing you, the ceremony, or anything else. They're worried about their own hair, dress, and good time too.

Savor the joy. You've done all you can to plan, prepare, and create the wedding of your dreams. Now it's time to relax, and concentrate on celebrating your marriage. Have a wonderful day!

Honeymoon Planning

It's good to get away after the wedding. That's why a honeymoon is such a popular tradition! It gives you both an opportunity to relax. You'll start your new life together without day to day distractions. No matter how limited your time and budget are, there are things you can do to make this time special. Try not to make it too complicated. If neither of you have ever traveled, a big trip around the world might overwhelm you both. Pick the type of honeymoon you want to have. Here are some things to talk about:

I want to travel
- [ ] as far away as possible.
- [ ] not too far from home.

I want to visit
- [ ] one destination.
- [ ] several destinations.

I like
- [ ] camping
- [ ] skiing
- [ ] hiking
- [ ] laying around
- [ ] big city sights
- [ ] beautiful scenery
- [ ] places of historical significance
- [ ] sunshine and beaches
- [ ] gambling and night life

I want to sleep in
- ☐ a luxury hotel.
- ☐ a country inn.
- ☐ a moderately priced motel.
- ☐ a cabin in the woods.
- ☐ a tent.

Before this
- ☐ I traveled extensively.
- ☐ I vacationed with my family as a child.
- ☐ I've been on a few short trips.
- ☐ we've traveled together.
- ☐ I've never traveled before.

We have
- ☐ a few days.
- ☐ a week.
- ☐ two weeks.
- ☐ unlimited time.
- ☐ no time.

BUDGETING THE HONEYMOON

Here are the costs to consider when you plan your expenses.

Transportation	$ _____	(gas, rental, tickets, tolls, parking)
Accommodations	$ _____	(sleeping facilities)
Meals	$ _____	(three a day, plus snacks)
Liquor	$ _____	(at dinner, places of entertainment)
Entertainment	$ _____	(admission, theater, golfing, etc.)
Gifts and Momentos	$ _____	(film, souvenirs)
Tips	$ _____	(at restaurants, hotels, taxis, airports, etc.)
Emergency Extra	$ _____	(car repair, illness, ruined clothes)
TOTAL	$ _____	

Because this should be a trip that you both enjoy, your final decision may have to be a compromise.

TIPS FOR A BETTER HONEYMOON

- Don't book on an airline that might go on strike around the time of your wedding, or visit a place that's been bothered by civil unrest.
- Make your arrangements and reservations early, especially if you'll be visiting a popular vacation spot during it's peak season.
- Obtain a written confirmation of arrangements. Bring your receipts with you. You'll have immediate proof if anything goes wrong.

- Convert most of your money to traveler's checks. Keep a list of their numbers, and the number you call to have them replaced, in a separate, safe place.
- Whenever possible you should use your credit card for purchases in foreign countries. In most cases you'll receive a better exchange rate.
- Label your luggage with name, address, and phone number both inside and outside.
- If you travel by plane, carry your personal essentials, and irreplaceable items, on board. Luggage can be lost and misplaced.
- Put a card in your wallet with the name and number of who to call in case of emergency. If you're both incapacitated, it'll help hospital personnel.
- Check the weather for that time of the year. You don't want to be there in the height of hurricane season, or driving through the mountains in a blizzard.
- If you're leaving the country, arrange for any shots and inoculations early. You don't want to be suffering from reactions on your wedding day. If you don't have a passport, make sure you both obtain one early. There's a waiting period. If you have one, make sure it's up to date.
- Take additional identification, such as driver's license and marriage certificate.
- Don't overpack. Try to take as many interchangeable items as possible. Choose clothing in similar styles and colors.
- Make sure monetary gifts from the wedding are deposited in the bank before you leave. If you won't have time, assign someone trustworthy to do the job. Endorse them "for deposit only" if you're worried.
- Leave a copy of your plans with family members in case they need to contact you in an emergency.
- Make sure to arrange for any rented items to be returned.
- Have someone check on your house or apartment every few days, and pick up your mail and newspapers. When the wedding announcement appears in the paper, prospective burglars might try to pay you a visit.
- Relax, have a good time, and don't let the little things get to you. This is your time to love each other and have fun. Enjoy.

Special Memories

This book was designed to help you keep everything for your wedding day in one handy place. When your wedding is over, you will have this book as a reminder of the many decisions that you made, and the many memories that you enjoyed! Take a few moments and fill in the blanks after your honeymoon—you'll be surprised how details fade over time.

Maid of Honor: _____

Female Attendants: _____

_____

_____

_____

_____

Flower Girl: _____

_____

Best Man: _____

Male Attendants: _____

_____

_____

_____

_____

Ring Bearer: _____

The Ceremony

Date _____ Time _____ Place _____

_____

Weather _____

Officiant _____

Decorations _____

_____

Special prayers or vows _____

_____

_____

_____

_____

_____

Music played _____

_____

Special guests _____

_____

_____

Moments to remember _____

_____

_____

145

Your Wedding Reception

Date _____ 147

Time _____ Place _____

_____

Menu _____

_____

_____

_____

Grace said by _____

Musicians _____

First song we danced to _____

Other special songs _____

Special guests _____

The garter was caught by _____

The bouquet was caught by _____

Moments to remember _____

_____

_____

A Bride's Message To Her Groom

The Secret to Making
Your Marriage Work

You have to get a good start. Believe me, it isn't as easy as you may think. Most divorces occur during the first few years of marriage. None of those couples thought it would happen to them either.

You want to be happy. What's the best way to go about it? How can *you* make *your* marriage last a lifetime? How do you avoid problems before they get out of hand?

You can learn everything you need to know from the hard-won experience of other married couples. They have already survived the blissful, but stormy days of early marriage.

In *NEWLYWED: A Survival Guide to the First Years of Marriage,* they share their secrets. They teach you how to make your marriage a lasting success. Open, friendly, and entertaining, this book offers a fascinating peek behind the closed doors of their married lives.

NEWLYWED will help you stop the fights that can destroy a relationship. It will show you the best way to create the marriage of your dreams.

Learn how to build the best possible life together from the beginning. You'll find an order coupon on the other side of this page. Send for your copy right away—and don't forget your friends!

Here are some practical, informative books that offer fresh insights and guidance during important times of your life. Don't forget your friends! Satisfaction guaranteed.

NEWLYWED: A Survival Guide to the First Years of Marriage
This friendly, open, and entertaining book is packed with practical advice from happily married couples. It covers a wide range of topics that will help you lay the groundwork for your new lives together. According to the Marriage Enrichment Association: "Taken seriously by a newlywed couple, this book could spell the difference between success and failure in their marriage." 256 pages $8.95

THE GROOM TO GROOM BOOK
A concise, informative, fun to read guide that will spark his interest in the wedding plans. Covers every topic from selecting rings to planning the reception. Includes advice, examples, illustrations, charts, worksheets, money-saving ideas, and much more. Will fully prepare him for an enjoyable wedding experience! 112 pages $7.95

BRIDE'S THANK YOU GUIDE
This popular guide to saying 'Thank You' makes the job both easy and fun. You'll find answers to questions regarding etiquette; and ideas, examples, and suggestions for writing warm, memorable notes that will please everyone who receives them. Includes over sixty sample letters dealing with every conceivable situation, and a mini-index for handy reference.

96 pages $4.95

THE BRIDE TO BRIDE BOOK
Since it's appearance on the wedding market, this book has become one of the most popular wedding planners available today. A complete wedding consulting service at an affordable price, it is packed with practical ideas, money-saving tips, examples, illustrations, and worksheets that will help you avoid problems, save money, and make the right decisions for a perfect wedding day. 160 pages $9.95

YOU CAN GO HOME AGAIN: The Career Woman's Guide to Leaving the Work Force
You'll probably think about leaving the work force at some point in time. It might be a way to spend more time with your children, or a period where you further your education. This book will help you make the decision, then ease you through a smooth transition. It includes wonderful tips for restructuring the family budget and making this move affordable. Booklist calls it "A thought-provoking and encouraging guide."

252 pages $9.95

153